W9-AKT-313

'O HORRABLE MURDER'

In loving memory of my father
Bernard Langworthy Partridge
1928 - 1998

and to all members past and present of
THE SEALED KNOT
in particular
Prince Maurice's Regiment of Dragoones.

'O HORRABLE MURDER'

The TRIAL, EXECUTION and BURIAL of
KING CHARLES I

ROBERT B. PARTRIDGE

THE RUBICON PRESS

The Rubicon Press
57 Cornwall Gardens
London SW7 4BE

© Robert B. Partridge, 1998

British Library Cataloguing in Publication Data

A catalogue record for this book is available from the
British Library

ISBN 0-948695-57-9 (hbk)
ISBN 0-948695-58-7 (pbk)

All rights reserved. No part of this publication may be reproduced, stored in a retrieval
system, or transmitted, in any form or by any means, electronic, mechanical, photo-
copying or otherwise, without the prior written permission of the copyright owners.

Designed by Peartree Design, Manchester.
Printed and bound in Great Britain by Biddles Limited of Guildford
and King's Lynn

Contents

List of Illustrations

Unless otherwise stated, all photographs and line drawings are by the author.

Cover: The effigy of Charles I in Madame Tussauds, London. Photographed with the permission of Madame Tussauds.

Title Page: The execution of King Charles I, after a contemporary illustration.

Back Cover: The Author.

Preface

Many scholarly books have been written on the English Civil Wars which led, ultimately, to the trial and execution of King Charles I on a cold January afternoon in 1649. The bibliography includes many books covering the reign of Charles I and the Civil War period.

My interest in the English Civil War is long-standing and, as you will gather from the dedication of this book, I am a member of the largest re-enactment society in the country - *The Sealed Knot.*

Founded in 1968 by a military historian, the late Brigadier Peter Young, the Society has now been re-enacting English Civil War battles and events for thirty years, a longer period than the original Civil Wars lasted. In addition to being great fun, the Society serves a *real* purpose, namely to educate the public who watch the re-enactments and also raise a considerable amount of money for charities up and down the country.

The many contemporary accounts of the battles and skirmishes of the Civil Wars are fascinating, but it is also essential to appreciate the key role of King Charles I. Once one understands the motives and thoughts of the King, the historical events can be put into their correct context.

I have always been fascinated by the contemporary accounts of the trial and execution of King Charles I. Especially interesting, and relatively unknown, is the story of the accidental rediscovery of his burial vault in the early years of the nineteenth century and the subsequent exhumation of the King's remains, which takes this story beyond the usual final date of 1649.

I have to thank many people for their assistance in collecting information for this book:

- Clive Alford, Assistant Administrator, The National Trust, Dunham Massey Hall, Cheshire.
- John Andrews Snr.
- Sarah Barter-Bailey, Librarian, Royal Armouries, H.M. Tower of London.
- The British Library, Newspaper Library.
- Rosemary Cooper, Acting Curator, Carisbrooke Castle Museum.
- Mrs. P. Copeman, St. George's Chapel Bookshop, Windsor Castle.
- Brian Haigh, Senior Museums Officer, Kirklees Museums and Galleries.
- Mrs Grace Holmes, Hon. Archivist, St. George's Chapel, Windsor.
- Brian Keith, Carisbrooke Castle.
- Julian W. S. Litten, Department of Prints and Drawings, Victoria and Albert Museum.
- Miss Jane Longton, Registrar, Royal Archives, Windsor Castle.
- I.F. Lyle, Sub-Librarian, Royal College of Surgeons of England.
- Madame Tussauds, London.
- Miss P. Rogers, Curator of Works of Art, Palace of Westminster.
- Ivan Roots, M.A.
- The Librarian, Hatfield House.
- The Secretary, National Association of Funeral Directors.
- The Museum of London.
- Christine Reynolds, Assistant Keeper of the Muniments, Westminster Abbey.

Finally I must especially thank:

- Peter Phillips who proof read my manuscript, designed the layout of this book and was always ready, as ever, with advice and practical help.
- Mrs Enid Davies, Assistant Archivist, St. George's Chapel, Windsor, for her help in locating archive material at Windsor.
- Dave Montford who processed my black and white films.
- Anthea Page, Juanita Homan and Robin Page, who are The Rubicon Press, for their support and encouragement.

INTRODUCTION

Almost three hundred and fifty years ago on a cold January afternoon, Charles Stuart, King of England, Scotland, Ireland and France stepped through a window of the Banqueting House in Whitehall onto a scaffold erected in the street. In front of a silent crowd, he was executed by the severing of his head from his body.

For the last few years of his life, the King was held prisoner by both Parliament and the Army. Contemporary accounts give us a vivid picture of his trial and last days.

The trial and subsequent execution of the King in 1649 amazed the whole of Europe. In the turbulent history of Great Britain, Kings had been killed before, had fallen victim to conspiracy and had been deposed and murdered. Charles's own grandmother, Mary Queen of Scots, had been tried and executed, but not when she was a reigning Queen and not in her own country and by her own subjects.

King Charles was brought to trial by his own people, an act which defied tradition and turned many long accepted religious values on their head. Even many who were against the King as a person, were in favour of the monarchy. The execution of the King, the subsequent abolishing of the monarchy and the establishment of a republic had great political repercussions.

Regardless of the rights and wrongs of Charles's actions before and during the English Civil War, the events of his last days show him to be a man who believed absolutely in his right to rule and in his ability to defend the laws and liberties of his people by his actions. Many contemporary and detailed accounts survive of the King's days as a prisoner and of his trial. Recorded by those who were opposed to him and his beliefs, these accounts show a man who went to meet his fate with a dignity and bravery which impressed friend and foe alike.

Charles was buried in an unmarked vault in St. George's Chapel at Windsor Castle. Normally that would be the end of the story, but Charles II had plans to build a new mausoleum for his father at Windsor.

Detailed designs were drawn up by Sir Christopher Wren, but for various reasons, which included the apparent inability to locate the vault which contained the body of Charles I, these plans came to nothing.

In the early years of the nineteenth century workmen accidentally broke into a vault in St George's Chapel and the coffin of King Charles I was found and opened, in the presence of the Prince Regent, later King George IV.

The exhumation revealed how the body of the King had been prepared for burial. Contemporary accounts of the funeral of the King show how simple it was, far different from what would have been expected of a royal funeral of this period. It is possible to compare and contrast the actual funeral arrangements of Charles I with the traditional royal funeral.

The story begins with the birth of a second son to King James VI of Scotland. It covers the period of the English Civil Wars which effectively ended in 1646 when the King was taken prisoner and subsequently tried and publicly executed. The story does not, however, end until 1888, when the Royal burial vault of Charles I at Windsor was opened for the last time, with the permission of Queen Victoria and in the presence of the Prince of Wales, later King Edward VII.

1999 sees the 350th Anniversary of the execution of King Charles I. The Civil Wars and the ultimate execution of a reigning sovereign changed forever the way the United Kingdom was to be governed. The basis of our Democracy today was established at this time of great unrest and unhappiness.

In his life and in the manner of his death, of all our line of monarchs, Charles I has perhaps had the greatest and the longest lasting impact on the way we live today. This is the story which follows...

I PRINCIPAL PLAYERS

In the following pages a number of historical characters will be mentioned. Some may be well known, but others may be new to some readers. A brief, biographical sketch is, therefore, given here, in chronological order, for some of the characters who play an important role in the unfolding story. The Bibliography includes many works where more detailed historical and biographical information can be found.

King Henry VIII: 1491-1547

Second son of King Henry VII, the founder of the Tudor Dynasty, Henry VIII was born at Greenwich in 1491, becoming King in 1509.

Henry inherited from his father a peaceful realm and an overflowing treasury. He was young and well educated and a man of strong will. If his servants did as he wished, he was a generous monarch and friend, but if they failed him, they were disposed of.

That his affections were volatile is perhaps best evidenced in his six marriages. The failure of his first marriage to Catherine of Aragon was ultimately to lead to the removal of the Pope as the head of the Church in England and the establishment of a "Church of England", of which the King was the head.

Two of his subsequent marriages ended with the execution of his queens: Anne Boleyn (number two) and Catherine Howard (number five).

The King created a subservient nobility to support him which he enriched with land confiscated from the monasteries he had dissolved. He was able to pass on a secure realm to his son, Edward VI, although the royal coffers had by this time been emptied.

Henry VIII is buried at Windsor in the same vault as his third wife, Jane Seymour, which also contains the body of King Charles I.

Queen Jane Seymour: 1509-1537

Born in Wiltshire, Jane Seymour met King Henry VIII whilst he was still married to his second Queen, Anne Boleyn. Jane was betrothed to the King the day after Anne's execution and was married to him a week later.

Henry already had two children, but no male heir, which he desperately wanted to ensure the continuance of the Tudor Dynasty. Catherine of Aragon had produced a daughter, later to be Queen Mary and Anne Boleyn another daughter, Elizabeth, later to be Queen Elizabeth I.

It was Jane Seymour who gave birth to the long-awaited heir, Edward, who later ruled briefly as King Edward VI. It was a difficult birth and two weeks later, the Queen died. She was buried at Windsor and is the only one of Henry's Queens to share his tomb.

King James I: 1566-1625

Son of Mary Queen of Scots and Henry Stuart, Lord Darnley, James was born in Edinburgh in 1566. A year after his birth he became King James VI of Scotland. As the senior member of the Royal House of Tudor (a grandson of Margaret, the eldest daughter of King Henry VII) James became the next in line to the English throne and became King James I of England on Elizabeth's death in 1603.

James was a small, awkward and ungainly man with a speech impediment. He firmly believed that Kings had a divine right to rule and that the Royal prerogative was unassailable. Because of this he quarrelled frequently with his Parliaments, who were seeking to increase their power.

After the reign of Elizabeth, Catholics were looking for more toleration of their religion and the Puritans for toleration of Presbyterianism. Both religious groups were to be disappointed. James appeared to favour the Catholics, but their cause ended with the infamous Gunpowder Plot of 1605. James survived the attempt to blow up the Houses of Parliament but lived the rest of his life in fear of assassination, particularly of explosions; his own father had been murdered this way when he was still a boy.

James did not add to his popularity by his coarse manners and he had the reputation of presiding over a corrupt and debauched Court. His favours towards the young Duke of Buckingham caused more unrest as did his aborted plans for the marriage of his son Charles I to the Catholic Infanta of Spain.

James's reign is notable for the persecution of witches and for his writings on the Divine Right of Kings and on the evils of tobacco.

Perhaps the greatest achievements of his reign were literary. These included the new translation of the Bible, the King James Version, which is still in use today, and the publication and performances of Shakespeare's plays.

James I is buried in Westminster, but does not lie with his Queen in the Stuart vault there. Either James (or perhaps his successor Charles I) decided that the founder of the Stuart dynasty should lie with his Tudor ancestor and the founder of the Tudor Dynasty, Henry VII.

Queen Anne of Denmark: 1573-1619

Anne, daughter of the King of Denmark, married King James VI of Scotland when she was fourteen years old. She was described as having golden hair, fair skin and was very tall. (Her height was not inherited by her children, but Charles II, her grandson, was also very tall).

Anne met her husband in Oslo; she had been travelling to Scotland but the weather deteriorated and she became stranded there. James impetuously travelled from Scotland to meet her. Their first winter together was spent in Denmark.

Anne had been provided with a substantial dowry which made her much more acceptable to James than any other potential brides. Nevertheless, the couple seemed well matched and were happy together, although the relationship settled into companionship in the last years. The marriage produced several children, only three of whom survived to maturity.

Anne was much criticised for her extravagance and for her love of pleasure, although art historians approve of her greatly for her patronage of the arts in England.

Queen Anne of Denmark is buried in Westminster Abbey.

Thomas Wentworth, Earl of Strafford: 1593-1641

Strafford was the principal and most influential of the advisers to King Charles I. He gained many enemies in Parliament and failed to strike first against them. Parliament impeached him on the grounds that he intended to create arbitrary government by bringing an Irish Army to England without their authority, and he was condemned to death.

Charles I failed to stand up against Parliament by exercising his right of veto against the sentence as Strafford had requested him to do. Strafford was subsequently executed in 1641 and is quoted as saying, "...put not your trust in Princes". The King was to regret this failure of decision for the rest of his reign.

William Juxon, Bishop of London: 1582-1663

Juxon was Lord Treasurer to Charles I from 1638 to 1641. He advised the King against the execution of Strafford.

1. William Juxon, Bishop of London. Portrait by an unknown artist in the National Portrait Gallery.

It was Juxon who attended the King during the last days of his imprisonment and during the trial. Juxon accompanied his King onto the scaffold and was present at the burial at Windsor.

Upon the Restoration of Charles II in 1660, Juxon returned to favour and Charles II made him Archbishop of Canterbury.

Oliver Cromwell: 1599-1658

Cromwell was a yeoman from Huntingdonshire.

The young Oliver was brought up as a typical Puritan gentleman and was educated at his local Grammar School, before studying at Sidney

2. Oliver Cromwell. Portrait by Robert Walker in the National Portrait Gallery.

Sussex College, Cambridge and at the Inns of Court.

At the age of twenty-four he was married to Elizabeth Bourchier, the daughter of a wealthy London furrier.

When he was twenty-nine he became Member of Parliament for Cambridge and was favoured by the Earl of Warwick, whose influence secured his rapid advancement, both political and military. With the dissolution of Parliament in 1629 he returned to his estates.

Cromwell was a man of great energy and he was passionately fond of outdoor sports. He played cricket and football in his youth and rode and hunted all his life.

He became strongly religious in his early thirties and believed passionately that he served God in all his actions.

When Parliament was recalled in 1640, he was again elected for both the Short and Long Parliaments as Member for Cambridge. He was a strong supporter of the action against Strafford.

During the Civil War he advanced through the ranks and became a competent and occasionally brilliant commander. Throughout his life he was always swift to act if he considered there was a need for it. At the start of the Civil Wars he heard that the Cambridge Colleges were about to sell their plate in order to raise money for the King. He moved quickly and seized the plate for Parliament.

After the Battle of Edgehill in 1642 he was promoted to Colonel. The Parliamentarian victory at Marston Moor in 1644 was achieved largely by his skill as a commander.

Cromwell greatly influenced the actions of the Army and Parliament in the events which led to the trial and execution of the King in 1649. He fought for liberty of conscience and freedom of worship. He had no doubt that an army inspired by such high ideals could not fail to be victorious.

After the execution of the King in 1649, the country was without a figurehead. In 1650, Cromwell replaced Sir Thomas Fairfax as Commander of the Army and became Lord Protector of the Realm from 1653. He was offered, but declined to accept, the Crown, although he took on the role of Monarch in all but name.

Cromwell was given a splendid funeral and burial in Westminster Abbey. After the Restoration of Charles II in 1660, his body was exhumed, dragged through the streets and hung at Tyburn. Later his head was displayed on a spike at Westminster. It now rests at Sidney Sussex College in Cambridge.

Sir Thomas Herbert: 1606-1682

Sir Thomas Herbert travelled widely, which was unusual for this period, and had visited the Middle East and India. When the Civil War began, he declared his support for Parliament.

Herbert was appointed by Parliament to attend King Charles I during the period of his captivity. Herbert became a Groom of the Bedchamber and despite his support of Parliament and his opposition to the policies and actions of Charles the King, he became close to Charles the man, and served him with great devotion until his execution in 1649. Herbert accompanied the body of King Charles I to Windsor and was present at the burial.

After the Restoration, Charles II rewarded Herbert for his service to Charles I by granting him a baronetcy.

3. Sir Thomas Herbert. Etching after a portrait by an unknown artist in the National Portrait Gallery.

Herbert kept diaries of his time with Charles I and in 1678 published the first draft of his memoirs.

John Bradshaw: 1602-1659

Bradshaw was a Cheshire lawyer, whose family home was at Marple Hall, near Stockport.

Bradshaw served as Lord President of the High Court of Justice raised to try Charles I. It was Bradshaw, in his capacity as President of the Court, who passed the sentence of death upon the King.

In March 1649, he became the first President of the Council of State, but was to fall from favour with Oliver Cromwell.

4. John Bradshaw. Portrait by an unknown artist in the National Portrait Gallery.

In 1661, two years after his death, his body was exhumed and exhibited in London in retribution for his part in the death of Charles I.

John Cook: 1608-1660

As Government Solicitor, it was Cook who prepared the charges against King Charles I and who acted as prosecutor at the trial. On the Restoration of Charles II in 1660, Cook was executed for his part in the death of Charles I.

Edward Hyde (later Lord Clarendon): 1609-1674

The Member of Parliament for Saltash, Hyde was implicated in the impeachment of Strafford. He became a famous, if not influential, adviser of King Charles I and for the period 1641 to 1645 was constantly at his side.

During the Commonwealth, Hyde was a strong supporter of the Restoration of the monarchy.

Hyde was created Lord Clarendon by Charles II in 1661. His daughter, Anne was married to the Duke of York, second son of Charles I and later to be James II.

As Lord Clarendon, he is chiefly remembered for his influential history of the Civil War. He began this work in Jersey in the period 1646 to 1648. The remainder of the work was written after the Restoration in 1660. His account of the Great Rebellion is still a fundamental source of information on the Civil War.

Henry Ireton: 1611-1651

Ireton was the Second in Command of the Horse of the New Model Army under Cromwell, whose son-in-law he was.

Member of Parliament for Appleby from 1645, Ireton was a staunch defender of private property, which he regarded as being fundamental to true liberty.

From 1648 he effectively directed the political moves of the New Model Army.

Ireton died whilst on active military service in Ireland, but his body was brought back to England for burial. After the Restoration, his body was exhumed and exhibited publicly, as punishment for his part in the death of Charles I.

Sir Thomas Fairfax: 1612-1671

Son of Ferdinando Lord Fairfax, Sir Thomas was second in command of the Parliamentarian Army in Yorkshire, which was under the command of his father.

In 1644 Sir Thomas was appointed Captain General of the New Model Army and in 1647 Commander of all the armed forces.

He became out of touch with the more radical elements of the Army and, in 1648, his authority was usurped by Cromwell.

Fairfax is said to have opposed the trial of the King, although he did nothing to prevent it. He gave up the command of the Army in 1650 in favour of Oliver Cromwell and withdrew from public life.

He was to prove a supporter of the Restoration of the monarchy under Charles II in 1660.

Prince Rupert: 1619-1682

Rupert was the second son of King Charles's elder sister, Elizabeth, by her marriage to Frederick, Elector of the Palatine.

Much of his youth was spent in military service during the Thirty Years War in Europe and he became an able officer.

At the outbreak of the Civil War he joined Charles I as his General of the Horse and was instrumental in the first Royalist victory at Powick Bridge in 1642.

5. Prince Rupert with his pet poodle "Boye" attacking Birmingham.

He fought at most of the major Civil War battles and gained a formidable reputation as a gifted soldier and cavalry leader.

Defeated at Marston Moor, the Prince's fortunes turned. He urged his uncle to make peace and was not in favour of the King's fighting the Battle of Naseby in 1645, which saw the Royalist cause destroyed.

Rupert's failure to hold Bristol, which he surrendered in 1644, led to his being cashiered by the King. He continued to fight for Charles's cause and became a naval commander.

Rupert spent the period of the Commonwealth in exile, and returned to England with King Charles II at the Restoration in 1660.

King Charles II: 1630-1685

Charles, Prince of Wales, was the eldest son of Charles I and Queen Henrietta Maria and was born at St. James's Palace in 1630.

Charles was an adolescent during the Civil War, in which he saw some military action. When his father was imprisoned, Charles fled to Holland where he was to remain in exile for some time.

After the execution of his father, Charles managed to return to Scotland, where, in January 1651, the Scots crowned him King. A new army was raised which marched into England, with Charles at its head. He reached as far south as Worcester, where he was proclaimed King of England. His sovereignty was short-lived, however, for his army was defeated at Worcester by a Parliamentarian force under the command of Oliver Cromwell on 3rd September 1651.

Charles managed to escape the field of battle and after an eventful flight across the country, during which he allegedly hid in an oak tree to avoid capture, he managed to escape to France, where he was to remain for the period of the Commonwealth.

In May 1660 the Monarchy was restored and Charles returned to England as King. At a ceremony held in the Banqueting House in London he was formally welcomed by both Houses of Parliament.

Charles had many mistresses and a number of illegitimate children but no legitimate heir. It was, therefore, his younger brother, James, Duke of York, who succeeded to the throne.

Charles modelled his Court on that of Louis XIV of France. His Court was lively after the sobriety of the Commonwealth and Charles earned the nickname of "The Merry Monarch".

It was during the reign of King Charles II that London was visited by the plague, which was followed in 1666 by the Great Fire of London. The destruction of much of the city enabled a great deal of rebuilding work to be undertaken, to replace the medieval slums with new buildings. This was the era of Sir Christopher Wren, whose work transformed the face of the capital.

Charles II died in 1685 having reputedly become a Catholic on his deathbed. He was buried in Westminster Abbey where his splendid funeral effigy is still to be found. The face of the effigy is based upon a death mask;

the tall figure is dressed in the oldest Garter Robes in Britain. When first displayed the effigy was described as, "...true to ye life and truly to admiration".

King James II: 1633-1701

Second son of King Charles I and Queen Henrietta Maria, James, Duke of York, was born at St. James's Palace in 1633. Much of his youth was spent abroad in exile during the period of the English Civil Wars and the Commonwealth.

After the Restoration of King Charles II in 1660, James returned to England. Charles II died with no legitimate heirs, and, despite earlier attempts by Parliament to exclude James from the throne because of his Catholic faith, he became King James II in 1685.

James's hunger for power and his open Catholic sympathies ultimately lost him his Kingdom.

A rebellion led by the Protestant Duke of Monmouth, illegitimate son of King Charles II, was severely put down in the year of James's Coronation. After Monmouth's execution, James began to pursue a more vigorous Catholic policy, ignoring the fear in the country that this policy generated.

James married twice. His first wife was Anne Hyde, daughter of Edward Hyde (Lord Clarendon). The two daughters of this marriage later became Queens: Mary (ruling jointly with William of Orange [William III]) and Queen Anne.

The King's second wife was Mary of Modena, a Catholic. When she produced a live male heir, the prospect of a line of Catholic Kings stretching into the future drove the Protestant Whigs to depose James and replace him with William and Mary. Following a bloodless coup in 1688, known as the "Glorious Revolution" James fled the country.

James died in exile in 1701 and is buried at St. Germain. His son, also called James, the "Old Pretender", continued to claim the title of the rightful King of England.

King George IV: 1762-1830

Eldest son of King George III, George was born at St. James's Palace in 1762.

During the later years of his father's reign he was made Regent for the King, who was ill with porphyria and considered unfit to reign.

George became King in 1821.

In his time as Prince Regent, George was noted for his extravagant lifestyle which did much harm to the monarchy.

George's political marriage to Caroline, the daughter of the Duke of Brunswick, was not a success. His treatment of her, particularly his refusal to allow her to enter Westminster Abbey to be crowned Queen, caused much discontent. The King had previously secretly married a widow, Mrs. Fitzherbert, but as she was a Catholic this union contravened the Royal Marriage Act and could not be acknowledged.

George IV is buried at Windsor.

King Edward VII: 1841-1910

Eldest son of Queen Victoria and Prince Albert, Edward was born at Buckingham Palace in 1841. In 1863 he married Alexandra, the daughter of King Christian IX of Denmark.

Throughout Queen Victoria's long reign, Edward was not given the freedom and responsibility he deserved as Prince of Wales. He was nearly sixty when he succeeded to the throne on the death of the Queen in 1901.

In his short reign he maintained good relations with foreign countries and contributed personally to maintaining peace.

Edward's undoubted charm and friendly personality won him much affection in a world which at this time was changing rapidly.

Edward VII is buried at Windsor.

II CHARLES STUART: FROM PRINCE TO PRISONER - 1600 TO 1646

On 24th March 1603, Queen Elizabeth I died and King James VI of Scotland succeeded to the English throne as James I. The union of the Crowns of England and Scotland under James was later celebrated by Charles I when he had Rubens provide the paintings for the ceiling of the new Banqueting House in London.

> Shake hands with Union, O thou mighty state
> Now thou art all Greate Britaine...
> No wall of Adrian serves to seperate
> Our mutuall love, nor our obedience,
> Being subjects all to one Imperial Prince.

Charles was born at Dunfermline Palace on 19th November 1600 the second son and youngest child of King James VI of Scotland and his Queen, Anne of Denmark. The new baby was weak and was not expected to live long.

When James succeeded to the English throne, he moved south with his Queen to London. Prince Charles, still a sickly baby, was left in Dunfermline in the care of nurses. Three years old, he was not yet able to walk and could not speak. In April 1604, an apothecary from London was sent to examine the Prince and determined that he was strong enough to be moved when the weather was warmer. In July the long journey south was made in short stages, with the Prince being carried in a curtained litter. His parents met him at Northampton.

The Prince was placed in the care of the wife of Sir Robert Carey. King James, concerned about the Prince's slow development, suggested that he might walk if his weak legs and ankles were placed in irons and that he might speak if surgeons cut the ligaments at the base of his tongue. Lady Carey assured everyone that this was not necessary and all that was needed was time and her care. The Prince spent a quiet childhood with the Careys, trying to walk without falling and to speak and be understood.

On 6th January 1605 Charles was created Duke of York by the King, the title reserved for the second son of the Sovereign. Charles sat at the head of the table in a special high chair at the feast prepared for the event. After this brief visit to the Court, he returned to the countryside where his health gradually improved.

By the age of eight the Prince was fluent in Latin and, whilst not as good a scholar as his elder brother, worked hard at his studies. He was still small for his age and pale, but he was able to walk well and his speech had improved significantly, although he was still troubled by a stammer. He retained a trace of a Scottish accent, which stayed with him for the whole of his life.

Charles grew up in the shadow of his elder brother, Prince Henry, who was six years older, having been born in 1594. He grew very close to his sister, Princess Elizabeth, who had been born in 1596.

The two brothers got on extremely well and Charles became devoted to Henry. There was no open rivalry between them. Charles seemed to know he could never achieve the successes of Henry, who did better at his lessons and was stronger and taller.

Charles's mother, Queen Anne of Denmark was a discerning collector and patron of the arts and greatly influenced the young Prince. Queen Anne patronised Inigo Jones, who as Surveyor of the King's Works designed for her the Queen's House at Greenwich, which was begun in 1616. Inigo Jones also designed the elaborate sets and costumes for the Court masques, performed in the Palace of Westminster. These masques often included members of the Court in various parts and Prince Charles made his first public appearance in arms in Ben Jonson's *Prince Henry's Barriers*, performed in the old Banqueting House at Whitehall in 1610.

Inigo Jones was also appointed Surveyor of Works to the Prince and fitted out a gallery for him to house his embryonic art collection. Charles, as Prince and later as Monarch, was to become one of the most discerning patrons and art collectors who has ever graced the British throne.

In 1612 Charles was suddenly and perhaps unhappily thrust into the limelight when he became heir apparent to the British throne, following the sudden death of Prince Henry. Henry had fallen ill with a mysterious fever, but refused to go to bed as he believed the best cure was physical exercise. After a game of tennis, he caught a chill and collapsed. The doctors could not agree on the cause of the Prince's illness (now believed to have been porphyria) and set about prescribing a variety of cures. These ranged from bleeding with leeches to applying a pigeon to his head. Henry's symptoms included headaches and buzzing in the ears. As he grew worse he became delirious and had convulsive fits. The doctors would allow no one from the royal family to visit the Prince; even the King was excluded. On 6th November the Prince, who was by then in a coma, died.

The family, and especially Charles, were devastated by Henry's death.

Only a few months after this tragedy, Charles was separated from his sister. Princess Elizabeth was now eighteen years old and had already had several suitors. The final choice of husband was dictated by politics and it was to strengthen the alliance with Protestant Germany that the Princess was betrothed to Frederick, the Elector of the Palatine. She was married in the February of 1613 and left for Germany. Charles had become deeply attached to Elizabeth and missed her greatly. He never saw her again.

6. Charles as Prince of Wales. Detail from a painting by Daniel Mytens at Montacute House, Somerset.

Charles was now on his own; his brother dead and his sister overseas. Queen Anne of Denmark had had other children, but they had all died as infants.

Charles had hitherto been kept in the background and was unprepared for the attention he now received. He was shy, still small in stature and retained a slight speech impediment which made him stutter on occasions and appear to stumble over his words. The Prince appeared to become detached and he withdrew into himself. His replies to questions were delayed and hesitant either from shyness or as if he was a slow thinker.

The Prince was, however, determined to succeed. He tried, albeit unsuccessfully, to cure his stammer by talking to himself with his mouth full of pebbles. A more successful ploy was to concentrate more on his words before he spoke.

Charles was haunted by the ghost of his brother, the popular and clever Prince Henry. Driven by determination, Charles concentrated on his lessons and eventually became a better scholar than his brother had been. He forced himself to be nearly as good a rider as Henry had been and he went running every morning in the park of St. James's Palace.

In November 1616, just before his sixteenth birthday, Charles was made Prince of Wales, the title previously held by his brother. His appearances at Court became more regular from this time, but to Charles it was more a duty than a pleasure, for he did not approve of the life and activities which took place there.

Various scandals had beset the Court, many of which involved his father the King. Charles seemed to be embarrassed by his father's coarse and often blasphemous jokes, by the apparent almost continual drunkenness of the Court and by the behaviour of those nearest the King. Charles felt isolated and not a part of the Court. To make matters worse for Charles, the King's main confidant was George Villiers, the second son of an impoverished Leicestershire squire newly arrived at Court, whom James elevated to the Peerage in instalments; George Villiers finally became the Marquis of Buckingham. Everyone, apart from the Prince of Wales, seemed to favour the young, attractive and intelligent rising star of the Court.

When Buckingham received his title of Marquis, Charles was nineteen. The Prince had reached his maximum height of five foot four inches. His continual exercise had overcome the weakness of his legs, which were, however, still slightly bowed. A delicate and refined figure, he was in great contrast to the King who was regarded as undignified and coarse. Charles did not, however, have the commanding presence of Buckingham. In his earlier years Charles had been compared continually with his brother; now comparisons were made between him and the popular Duke of Buckingham.

Charles initially showed a petulant resentment of the Duke but, ultimately, was unable to resist his disarming personality. Before long the two young men were often in each other's company and became friends rather than rivals.

The death of the Prince's mother, Queen Anne, at Hampton Court in March 1619 was greatly to strengthen his friendship with the Duke. During the last years of the Queen's life, when she was troubled with illness, the Prince grew close to her. He was with her when she died and was deeply affected by this. Thereafter the Prince turned increasingly to Buckingham for advice and support.

As Charles warmed to the Duke of Buckingham, the rest of the Court and the country grew concerned at his influence over the King and affairs of the realm. Queen Anne's estate came into the King's possession and he bestowed a large part of it on Buckingham who had also been given many official appointments, Master of the Horse and Lord High Admiral to name but two. The result of this was that the Duke had little time, or perhaps inclination, to give any of the positions the time they needed to solve problems or direct affairs effectively. Charles, however, oblivious to all this, became devoted to the Duke.

James was at this time experiencing political problems and ones which were to bring him directly into conflict with Parliament. As Charles was to learn, it was essential for Parliament to be called periodically, for it was only Parliament who could provide money. James disliked Parliament and had remarked in private that he was surprised that his "ancestors should have permitted such an institution to come into existence."

The Catholic armies of Spain and Austria had invaded the Palatine and forced James's daughter Elizabeth to flee. There was great clamour from the public to defend the Protestant Princess, known popularly in England as the "Queen of Hearts", and action was demanded against Spain and Austria. When Parliament was summoned in 1621 to provide funds for the King's foreign policy, it advocated a war against Spain.

James, however, had other ideas. He had made peace with Spain soon after coming to the throne and now sought to cement that alliance, and also receive a large dowry, by arranging for Charles to marry the Spanish Infanta, Donna Maria.

The King came into direct conflict with Parliament who would have nothing to do with a Catholic marriage. James would not accept that Parliament had a right to question his policy and dissolved it.

The negotiations for the marriage proceeded, in the hope that Spain would support the return of the King's daughter and son-in-law to the Palatine.

The Infanta was devastated at the idea of marrying a Protestant and declared she would rather go to a monastery. Charles believed that his sister's cause, his father's wishes and his country's future should overcome his own feelings. Once resolved on this course of action, the Prince appeared so keen on the liaison, that it almost seemed as if he had fallen in love.

Charles left for Spain, in the company of the Duke of Buckingham, determined to win the Princess's heart. In Spain the Prince and the Duke were lavishly entertained, although it was some time before the Prince and the Infanta were allowed to meet. On that occasion, Charles rejected the formal speech which had been prepared for him and blurted out his love for her in words which amazed the Court. Only the Infanta was unmoved; perhaps she realised her suitor's hopes would never be realised. The negotiations foundered quickly over religious matters. It was clear that Charles would not be permitted to marry the Infanta unless he renounced his religion and made major concessions to Catholics in England in his father's name. The Pope became involved and discussions touched on the religious upbringing of any children of the proposed marriage.

Throughout this, Charles seemed frustrated and thwarted and declared that the other girls he had seen were "as nothing to her." Charles feared the prospect of returning to England with his mission a failure and tried to win her by deceit. He made a host of promises about the future of English Catholics which he convinced the Spanish that Parliament would adopt. Buckingham flew into a rage after hearing of the impossible proposals and determined that they should leave Madrid as soon as possible.

Back in England, James formally accepted Spanish terms, defying the immense opposition. Further delays followed when the Pope died and the marriage could not proceed until a new Pope was elected. Spain then showed little interest in actually assisting the return of the Protestant Elector to the Palatine, which was a major part of the marriage agreement. Petty squabbles between the English delegation in Spain over religion complicated matters still further. Charles finally realised that Buckingham was right and they returned to England.

Charles and Buckingham were given a warm welcome home, and the country was relieved to find out that the rumours that Charles had been duped into marrying the Infanta and had embraced the Catholic faith, were ill-founded.

There was still some pro-Spanish support and one leading public servant, the Earl of Middlesex, stated that the Prince was duty-bound to marry the Infanta. Persuaded by Buckingham, James called a Parliament, which could impeach Middlesex on the familiar charge that as a Treasury Official he had misappropriated funds and amassed a vast personal fortune.

Parliament was recalled, Middlesex impeached and Parliament again advocated a hostile stand against Spain. In the preparations for war against Spain, new allies were sought, which now included France. Marriage negotiations with Spain were now formally ended.

7. James I greets Prince Charles on his return from Spain.

Charles had matured greatly during his visit to Spain. His close association with Buckingham had turned the shy boy into a more confident and self assured young man.

"He is grown a fine gentleman," a contemporary wrote,

"...and beyond all expectation I had of him when I saw him last, which was not these seven years; and, indeed I think he never looked nor became himself better in all his life."

James now looked to France to provide a bride for the Prince. The chosen princess was fourteen years old. Her name was Henrietta after her father Henri IV of France, who had been murdered when she was just a few months old, and Maria after her mother, Marie de Medici.

The Princess was small and dark and walked about with the quick and sudden movements of a sparrow. She spoke quickly and had a fiery temper. Only the most extravagant of her admirers called her beautiful, but her personality and vivacity made her far from plain.

Portraits were exchanged and the negotiations for the marriage progressed, but were interrupted by the death of King James.

At fifty-eight, James had been unwell for some time. He had lost most of his teeth and bolted his food, which gave him chronic indigestion. His love of fruit, to excess, often gave him diarrhoea. His doctors also diagnosed arthritis, nephritis and colic. The King was always scratching himself, fiddling with his codpiece and belching. His over-padded clothes, worn as a precaution against assassins, made him too hot and when he threw off his outer garments, he frequently caught chills.

Red urine and sensitive skin were more ominous signs of his illness, which suggest that, like his son Prince Henry, James suffered from porphyria.

After his death the surgeons opened the body and found all the vitals "...were sound as also his head, which was very full of brains; but his blood was wonderfully tainted with melancholy."

Porphyria is now known to be hereditary and it was through James's daughter, Elizabeth, that the disease was passed down the generations into the Hanoverian Royal House in the next century. George III suffered from porphyria, which at the time was mistaken for madness.

After the accession of Charles to the throne, the marriage negotiations with France continued despite some public opposition to another proposed Catholic marriage. As part of the formal agreement with France, Charles agreed to allow English Catholics some freedom of worship. The future Queen was told she would be allowed to continue her faith and that she would be allowed to educate any children until they were thirteen years old. She would be allowed her own chapel, and chaplains. All her private attendants were to be French and Catholic.

The marriage was celebrated at Notre Dame Cathedral in Paris on May Day, 1625, with the Duc de Chevreuse standing in for the absent Charles. The Duke of Buckingham was sent to France to escort the Queen to England and she arrived in June, when her second wedding took place at Canterbury on the 14th, this time with her husband beside her. Two days later they set out for London, their route lined by cheering and waving crowds.

Charles had been enchanted by the Princess and had every hope that the marriage would turn out well. Henrietta, however, soon decided that she did not like England and, surrounded by her Catholic entourage, she seemed to flaunt her Catholicism, to the annoyance of those not of that faith.

Charles was crowned King at Westminster Abbey in 1625. The event was seen by him not as a great event of state, but as a sacred and almost private ceremony. At the coronation, the King broke with the tradition of wearing purple robes and was dressed completely in white. The Queen did not attend, nor was she ever formally crowned as Queen.

Henrietta became homesick. She had made no attempt to learn English and she showed no inclination to talk to anyone apart from the French women who were her constant companions. Charles was convinced that her unhappiness was caused by the presence of the Catholic priests and consequently ordered nearly all her French ladies, servants and priests to leave the country. The state of the marriage worsened as a result of this action.

Charles took his Kingship very seriously and was determined to become a truly great King. He was quieter and more reserved than both his late father and his brother and he deliberately cultivated distance and the dignity of the monarchy.

He felt it was his duty to uphold the two basic principles of his life: his prerogative as King and his religion. He was uninterested and untrained in politics and his failure to learn quickly the art of government was to prove his downfall.

The Court at Whitehall was made the most formal and elegant in Europe by the new King. Charles's own taste was impeccable and he created around him a setting worthy of him as King of a great and important country.

Charles was a splendid patron of the arts and commissioned paintings of the royal family and members of the court by Van Dyck. Rubens provided paintings for the ceiling of the new Banqueting House in London, the building of which had been completed in 1619. Ben Jonson became his Poet Laureate and wrote masques for the Court to perform. Charles had plans to replace completely the old and rambling Palace of Westminster, most of which never came to fruition.

Charles fitted perfectly into the ordered setting of his Court. Gone was the vulgarity and coarseness of the Court of James I. The King's shyness and his sense of being an anointed King kept him apart from most people.

If the King was distant to his Court, to his subjects he was even more remote. Apart from regular visits to Scotland, before the outbreak of the

8. King Charles I. Portrait by, or after, Sir Antony Van Dyck at Dunham Massey House in Cheshire.

Civil Wars, Charles rarely travelled his kingdom. Most of his time was spent in his various palaces in the Home Counties where he indulged his passion for riding and hunting.

Charles appeared aloof and cold and with little or no sense of humour. He failed to make any real impression on those whom he received in audience.

Meanwhile the war with Spain was progressing badly, being inadequately funded and ill equipped. Before the war (known as the Thirty Years War) ended, England had drifted into war with France too. The dismissal of Henrietta Maria's French servants had not helped good relations between the two countries.

In 1626, a force under the Duke of Buckingham set out to relieve the French town of La Rochelle, where Protestant Huguenot rebels were under seige by the Catholic troops of the French King. Buckingham tried, unsuccessfully, to starve a nearby French force into submission. When French reinforcements arrived, Buckingham's army was badly mauled and he was obliged to retreat, having incurred a great deal of expense, much loss of life and no result. Parliament saw this as their chance to remove Buckingham and set out to ruin him. The King remained Buckingham's only friend. The Duke was blamed for the disastrous policies of the King, and Parliament determined to accuse Buckingham of High Treason. The King's swift response was to dissolve Parliament.

James I had always asserted that, as King, he was above or outside the law and that he had no duty to communicate with Parliament. In practice, however, he was in almost constant contact with it. Charles on the other hand could not manage Parliament and therefore ignored it. He had no doubt that it was Parliament's duty to recognise his absolute authority and he would not be forced by them to comply with legal obligations which in his opinion did not exist.

Buckingham was safe for the time being, but Charles was now unable to raise money for the war with France through the Commons. He imposed new duties and taxes, but ultimately was forced to recall Parliament. Parliament refused to grant funds until the King acknowledged their complaints about his conduct and unlawful raising of taxes without their consent. They reached an uneasy compromise which saved Buckingham from further attack.

The King stated that:

"...the people's liberties strengthen the King's prerogative and that the King's prerogative is to defend the people's liberties...if Parliament have not a happy conclusion the sin is yours. I am free of it."

The feeling of the people against Buckingham was still strong. In August, Buckingham was getting ready to lead another relief force to La Rochelle. There had been many threats made against the Duke's life and at Portsmouth he was attacked by one of his former officers, one John Felton.

Felton had no difficulty in getting into the Duke's house and when Buckingham was called away from his meal Felton took his chance and plunged a dagger into the Duke's left breast. Buckingham pulled the dagger from his chest and staggered into the hall of the house, trying to unsheathe his sword, crying, "The villain hath killed me!" He collapsed on a nearby table, blood pouring from his mouth and died in the arms of a doctor.

Charles was at his prayers when the news reached him. He was devastated and went to his room where he threw himself across his bed, sobbing uncontrollably. He remained in the room all that day. Buckingham had been his closest and only friend. No one would replace him.

Charles threw himself into his work, which perhaps was the only cure to his grieving, although whenever he could he retired into quiet domesticity. His marriage had got off to a shaky start, but what had started as an arranged marriage, turned out to be blissfully happy.

The Queen, Henrietta Maria, but known to the King and subjects as Mary, was a small delicate figure. She was intelligent and resolute, with a flair for statecraft and showed a shrewdness inherited from her father Henri IV of France and her mother's family, the Medici.

The Queen was the only person in whom the King confided after the murder of Buckingham, and it was inevitable that she influenced his thoughts and actions. In any other country, apart from England, this influence would have been regarded as perfectly normal and perhaps even beneficial. The Queen was however a Catholic, and as such, much of her supposed advice to the King was regarded by many of his subjects with great suspicion.

Like Charles, Henrietta Maria was a poor judge of character and favoured those whom the nation mistrusted. The people she should have trusted were those who were too Protestant to be at ease in her company. The Queen favoured people because of their services. Charles, on the other hand, took other people's services for granted. To him, it was no more than every subject owed to their anointed King. Servants could be dismissed at a moment's notice and then forgotten. To those considered to be his friends, however, he could be extremely faithful.

The Queen was soon pregnant and on 13th May, 1629, a baby boy was born at Greenwich Palace. It was a difficult birth and Charles urged

9. Queen Henrietta Maria.
Portrait by, or after, Sir Antony Van Dyck at Dunham Massey House in Cheshire.

that at all costs the life of the Queen be saved. The baby, weak and small, died shortly after its christening. The Queen recovered.

By October the same year, the Queen was pregnant again. On May 29th 1630, another baby boy was born, but this time he was big and healthy, even if, as she admitted, he was an ugly baby. The boy was christened Charles. Other children followed: Mary, born the next year, James in 1633, Elizabeth in 1635, Anne in 1637, Henry 1640 and Henrietta in 1644. Another daughter died within a few moments of birth.

The King and Queen, the years of unhappiness behind them, settled down to a contented family life. Charles did as little work as he could and had neither the taste or talent for administration, preferring to leave that to his ministers. Hours, which should have been spent governing, were spent instead at tennis, bowls, golf, swimming, hunting, theological discussions and in guiding selected visitors around the splendid art treasures of his palaces.

One of his main entertainments was the Court masque: allegorical and historical plays with music and dance, in which he and the Queen often played the principal parts. Extravagant sets and costumes were prepared for these performances, which were usually held in the Banqueting House, with members of the Court and invited dignitaries as the audience.

Charles was now convinced that his political problems were over. Parliament, disbanded in 1629, was not to be called for another eleven years. The War with Spain and France had ended, which meant that the King was able to pay his way without having to ask a Parliament for funds. During this period, the King and his ministers resorted to a number of devices, some of dubious legality, to raise taxes. Many people were resentful and unhappy with this.

Although Charles had no First Minister after Buckingham, nor any other close friends, the nearest person to fulfil this role was Thomas Wentworth, later created Earl of Strafford. He was the most able of the King's servants, but never managed to fill the role of friend to the King. Strafford was exactly the sort of minister the King needed, strong and able. With such a minister, Charles could have become a popular and successful monarch. This was not to be however, and much of Strafford's work for the King kept him in either York or Dublin and away from the Court.

The raising of taxes without Parliament, and with the assistance of Strafford, caused more and more unrest. Religious matters caused concern too. William Laud, Archbishop of Canterbury, overworked, fussy and often rude and outspoken, made many verbal attacks on the Puritans within the Anglican Church. Laud was determined to restore to the Church some of the wealth lost during the Reformation. He also sought to make churches more beautiful, to introduce conformity in the use of the prayer book, to replace the Communion Table as an altar at the east end of the church and to make the services orderly with more ritual and vestments. To many, this smacked of Popery and Catholicism. It was Scotland who rebelled first when Laud tried to introduce a new prayer book along the Anglican lines. There was a riot in St. Giles's Cathedral in Edinburgh. The Scots wanted to restrict the bishops' power and they expressed their aims in a National Covenant. Before long an army was raised. Negotiations commenced but faltered. The King tried to raise an army, but there was little enthusiasm for it and even less money. At Berwick in 1639, before any blows were struck, the King made his peace, agreeing that the Scottish Parliament and Assembly should settle the matter. This did not work as the King refused to allow his bishops to be controlled by the Assembly. The Scottish Parliament was dissolved and conflict seemed inevitable.

The King and the Queen now realised that perhaps Strafford was needed to control the situation. He was too masterful and forthright for their tastes, but at a time like this, was the one man who could perhaps save the day. Strafford was recalled from Ireland.

Strafford's advice was for direct and decisive action against the Scots, a policy which had brought some stability to Ireland. The rebellion in Scotland must be crushed and to raise the funds, Parliament must be called.

Parliament assembled, but did not automatically agree funds for the conflict. The new Parliament, which had not sat for eleven years, proved difficult over the granting of supplies and there were reports that they were in negotiations with the Scots rebels.

Strafford and Charles were appalled by this and there was little alternative but for the Parliament to be dissolved again.

The problem of the Scots still remained and if Parliament would not vote funds to raise an army in England, other action had to be taken. Strafford pointed out that the King already had an army in Ireland and told Charles "You may employ them here to reduce this kingdom."

An ill-equipped and underpaid army was raised by the King in England, without having to use the Irish Army as Strafford had suggested. Charles and Strafford, who was suffering from dysentery, went North, to meet the rebel army who had advanced into England. The King and Strafford soon realised that the enterprise was doomed to failure from the start. A humiliating peace was agreed with the Scots. The rebels were allowed to remain in Northumberland and Durham, with their army being paid until their compensation claims were settled by the English Parliament.

Charles once again was obliged to call Parliament. The members were now determined they would not let the King dismiss them so quickly and there was a strong move to remove Strafford, the King's latest "evil counsellor". Strafford was arrested on the charge of treason and sent to the Tower of London.

Strafford was tried in Westminster Hall and conducted his own defence with great skill. The charge of High Treason was difficult for the court to prove and Strafford continually scored points over those who would prosecute him. Parliament was determined not to lose its prey and determined that if a charge of High Treason could not be proved, all that was needed was a Bill of Attainder. Such a bill would declare Strafford's execution necessary for the safety of the country.

When the Act of Attainder for the death of Strafford came before the House of Lords, Charles declared that he would never give it the Royal Assent. The Lords, nonetheless, proceeded to pass the Bill, to avoid the wrath of Parliament and the populace, convinced the King would keep his word and save Strafford. Charles, however, went back on his promise and was scared into signing the death warrant by the fury of the London mob, whom, he believed, were a threat to the safety of the Queen and his children.

The King knew that he had sacrificed an innocent and able servant and his decision was to cause him much regret in the years to follow. When news of the execution reached Cardinal Richelieu, in France, he declared, "...they have killed their wisest man."

Parliament, not content with having successfully removed Strafford, also had Archbishop Laud arrested and sent to the Tower of London, where he was held a prisoner. The King was then presented by Parliament with a host of demands which would have resulted in a reduction in the accepted powers of the monarchy and an increase in their own powers. The *Grand Remonstrance* was a detailed list of complaints, grievances and requirements of Parliament. Parliament also demanded that bishops be deprived of their votes in the House of Lords.

Charles refuted the *Remonstrance*, denied that he had any evil advisers and refused to accept that there was any need to reform the church.

Charles now made his greatest political blunder when Parliament attempted to impeach the Queen. To prevent this, Charles attempted to arrest five members of the House of Commons who were the most vociferous in their verbal attacks on the Queen. The charge against them was to be one of treason.

The Queen urged the King to show his enemies that he was master in his own kingdom. She threatened to leave him if he did not, "...go and pull those rogues out by the ears."

Charles descended upon Parliament in person, accompanied by four hundred armed troops. He boldly entered the House of Commons, which was in session, accompanied by Prince Rupert. The soldiers took their stations outside the chamber.

Charles walked towards the Speaker's chair, nodding to members he recognised as he passed.

"Mr Speaker," he said, "by your leave, I must for a time make bold with your chair."

Seated in the Speaker's chair, the King explained his presence in the Chamber and asked for the five members in question to come forward. There was no response from the silent House. The King asked the Chamber if Pym, one of the five members he sought, was there and when he received no reply asked the same question of the Speaker.

"Sire," the Speaker replied, "I have neither eyes to see nor tongue to speak in this place but as the House is pleased to direct me."

"'Tis no matter," replied the King. "I think my eyes are as good as another's".

The King examined the benches in the House, but the five members had already fled to safety, having been warned in plenty of time of the King's intentions.

"Well," said the King, "since I see all my birds have flown, I do expect that you will send them unto me as soon as they return hither."

By the time the King returned to Whitehall, London was in an uproar. Charles refused to be intimidated and issued a proclamation for the arrest of the five.

Rumours abounded that supporters of the King planned to attack the city of London and hang Pym. Barricades were erected and preparations for the expected conflict were made. On 11th January, Pym and his fellow wanted men came out of hiding and sailed openly in a triumphant procession on the river to Westminster where they were met by cheering citizens. No attempt was made to arrest them as the King had ordered.

The King had, in fact, already left London and was at Hampton Court. Later the family travelled to Windsor. The Queen left for Holland, taking with her some of the Crown Jewels which she planned to use to raise money for the King's cause.

Parliament and the King were now in opposite corners; London was lost to him and possibly the Home Counties too. Both the King and Parliament attempted to gain control of the militia; Parliament wanted to ensure that all the armed forces and the authority to raise new troops were under its control. Charles refused to allow Parliament to control the Army.

Parliament passed the *Militia Ordinance* without the King's Assent. Charles was in York at this time. In May 1642 the King issued a proclamation forbidding the militia to comply with the *Ordinance*, but Parliament went ahead and raised the troops. Charles was now obliged to meet force with force.

Supporters rallied to his cause and the King raised his battle standard in Nottingham in 1642.

10. The raising of the King's Standard at Nottingham in 1642.

The Standard was unfurled under a gloomy sky and in a strong wind. A formal proclamation declaring the Commons and its troops as traitors had been prepared. At the last moment the King altered the wording which resulted in his Herald being hardly able to read the Proclamation. Later, in the strong wind, the Standard was blown down.

The thought of Civil War filled the King with horror, but he was reluctant to make offers of peace to Parliament, which his advisors urged him to do. Eventually he did approach Parliament, the action reducing him to tears and making him so overwrought that he could not sleep. Parliament refused the peace offer unless the King withdrew his protection from those of his supporters who had "...been voted by both Houses to be delinquents." The Queen feared that the King would abandon his supporters and forgive his enemies and once again urged him to stand firm, which he did.

The first battle of the Civil War was fought at Edgehill in October of the same year, but the result of the encounter was inconclusive. The King, however, made the mistake of being too considerate towards his enemies and he failed to follow up any advantage he may have gained by the battle. Prince Rupert, the King's nephew, proposed an immediate march to London, which at that time was virtually undefended. The King's advisers told him that if Rupert reached London before him, with an army, that the hot-headed prince would "set the town afire". Charles delayed any action, by which time any chance of success had evaporated.

The King's second strategic error was to urge Prince Rupert to fight the Scots and the army of Parliament at York in 1644. At the battle of Marston Moor, Rupert's army was soundly defeated. Charles was at this time beset with personal problems, as the Queen was gravely ill following the birth of a daughter and was not expected to live. (The baby, Princess Henrietta, and the Queen both survived.)

In 1645 the King's decision to fight at Naseby was his third strategic error. His advisers, including Prince Rupert, all advised against it. The Queen added her voice and argued against Rupert. The battle of Naseby saw the utter defeat of the King and the effective end of his cause, even though the Civil War still rumbled on for almost a year.

If the King was not a good strategist, he did at least prove to be an able and brave soldier in the heat of battle. Winters were spent in Oxford, but in the campaigning season, Charles spent much of his time with his troops, sharing their hardships and dangers. His superb horsemanship stood him in good stead and he took part in several major engagements, including two Royalist victories at Copredy Bridge and Lostwithiel, both in 1644.

In battle, Charles very much directed operations himself and after the fighting, he rode the field issuing orders that the defeated enemy was not to be plundered.

At Edgehill, in a black cloak with the Star of the Garter on his chest he "...rode along the lines encouraging his men." At Naseby, in his gilt armour, he tried to lead his troops personally in one final charge which might have saved the day. At the last moment, the Earl of Carnworth, riding next to the King, seized the bridle of the King's horse and turned the animal's head.

"Will you go upon your death in an instant?" shouted the Earl, along with, "...two or three full-mouthed Scot's oaths." The troop of horse following the King took this as a sign that they should also turn and before Charles fully realised what was happening, they had galloped away. The moment and the battle was lost.

In addition to the military defeat of Naseby, Charles's personal papers and correspondence were seized by Parliament. These revealed his plans and were later to be used in evidence against him at his trial.

Charles had lost the war, but nevertheless had gained some considerable increase in his stature as a man, although opinion had polarised into two distinct groups: those who saw him as a "man of blood" and those who saw him as a hero.

The Civil War brought him into contact with great numbers of his subjects and more people than before felt an intense loyalty to him which had previously not existed. Few of his followers deserted him as his fortunes declined. Indeed many new supporters rallied to his cause, even after his military defeat.

The War had caused great distress and hardship to the King's subjects. Communities and family loyalties were divided between the causes of King and Parliament. Some who rallied to their chosen cause did so from a genuine desire to fight for their beliefs and rights, but many who lost their lives were involved because they had no real free choice in the matter. Troops of soldiers were raised by wealthy landowners and the nobility, and able-bodied men were effectively conscripted into one army or the other.

The military activities left a trail of devastation and grief which touched all parts of the country. The conflict affected civilians as well as soldiers. The armies had to be equipped, fed and housed and the drain on the country's economy and the disruption to normal business and trade was immense.

Despite defeat, Charles had not given up hope. The victors were still at this time in favour of a monarch and some were more sympathetic to him following his defeat. Negotiations began, but ultimately foundered because of Charles's absolute refusal to budge from his basic principles. Had he been willing to bend on his ideas of his religion and his role as a Monarch, then he might have preserved his life. Even the Queen was unable to shake his resolve on these points. The end was inevitable.

III   IMPRISONMENT

When, in the Summer of 1642, Charles Stuart, King of England, raised his battle standard at Nottingham, his subjects were divided in their loyalties; there were those who supported the King and those who supported Parliament. The King's opponents had believed that once they were victorious in the field of battle, the King would readily give way to their demands. It was hoped that Parliament would be consulted by the King in his choice of Ministers and would take over the control of the Army. Parliament had also wanted the King to reform the Church, abolish bishops and make Parliament the ultimate authority in all ecclesiastical matters.

These changes would have transformed Parliament from a purely advisory body to the King, which is what it had always been, to the governing power of the nation, which is what it wanted to be.

In this new world, the King would remain as a figurehead, but the real power, civil, military and ecclesiastical would be exercised by the House of Commons, whose members were the gentry, lawyers and merchants of the country. The Commons would be strengthened by the House of Lords, whose influence was already well established.

The King would, it was thought, be agreeable to such terms as the price for peace in the country and his own freedom.

Parliament was wrong in making these assumptions. It had not allowed for the King's absolute and steadfast belief that God had given him the authority to rule. To relinquish any part of this authority was viewed by him as a sin. He was prepared to risk his freedom and life (and the lives of his subjects) to keep intact his sacred authority and to be able to hand over that authority in due course to his son.

The first Civil War ended early in 1646 when the King's remaining forces were defeated at Stow-on-the-Wold; the war had ended, but it was not yet followed by a firm peace. In May of that year Charles rode into the camp of the Scottish army, which was besieging Newark, and surrendered to its Commander.

Charles's army had been effectively defeated at Naseby the previous year and most of his experienced officers and soldiers had been killed or were in prison. The King knew that there was no prospect of raising a new army capable of defeating the victorious Army of Parliament, but he hoped that he could manipulate to his advantage the various factions which were against him. The Scots distrusted the English Parliament, and Parliament suspected the motives of the Scots and feared the power of the English army.

The King was taken to Newcastle-upon-Tyne where he entered into negotiations with the Scots. The negotiations failed, as Charles would have nothing to do with Presbyterianism, acceptance of which was essential for any agreement with the Scots.

At this stage the King was still hoping that he would be able to negotiate with Parliament. When, therefore, he received a proposition from Parliament, which included his acceptance of their control over the Army, he replied requesting that he be allowed to travel to London to pursue the talks. He was evidently concerned about his safety and asked for a guarantee:

> "Upon the security of the two Houses of Parliament and the Scots Commissioners that he shall be there with freedom, honour and safety. Where by his personal presence he may not only raise a mutual confidence between him and his people, but also have these doubts cleared, and these difficulties explained unto him, which he now conceives to be destructive to his just regal power."

Charles was clearly hoping to play for time, but the Scots, realising that he would never change his views, handed him over to the English Parliament in February 1647. He was lodged at Holdenby House in Northamptonshire, under a Parliamentarian Commander, Richard Graves.

The Army wanted to negotiate directly with the King and was also concerned that there might be attempts to rescue him. A troop of horse, commanded by Cornet Joyce, was sent to seize the King. Joyce's written orders stated:

> " ...Wee souldiers now under his Exellency, Sir Thomas Fairfax his command, have by one general consent of the souldiery manifested our true love to the Parliament and kingdome by endeavouring to prevent a second warr, discovered by the designement of some men privately to take away the king, to the end he might side with that intended army to be raised, which if effected would be the utter undoing of the Kingdom."

The King asked Joyce by what authority he was to be moved.

Joyce told him,

"I am sent by the authority of the Army , to prevent the design of their enemies, who seek to involve the kingdom a second time in blood."

"That is no lawful authority. I know of none in England but mine, and after that of the Parliament," replied the King. The discussion along these lines continued until Joyce said to the King, "I beseech your Majesty to ask me no more questions. There is my commission!" Joyce turned and indicated the soldiers behind him.

The King replied with a smile,

"I never before read such a commission, but it is written in characters fair and legible enough...But to move me from hence you must use absolute force, unless you give me satisfaction as to those reasonable and just demands which I make; That I may be used with honour and respect and that I may not be forced in any thing against my conscience or my honour...You are masters of my body, my soul you cannot reach."

Joyce was able to report to Cromwell that he had "...secured the King."

Charles seemed ready enough to go with the Army as his talks with Parliament had failed. A contemporary wrote,

"I believe his Majesty had no reason to be very fond of the place where he was before, or of the great respect he received there."

Charles was moved to the military headquarters of the Army at Newmarket, a place chosen by him, where the Army presented its terms, which included keeping the Church of England, tolerating all Protestants and giving Parliament control of the Army. Charles was evasive in his reply, hoping perhaps to play Parliament and the Army one against the other and, thereby, recover as much of his power as possible.

When Parliament seemed ready to re-open negotiations with the King, the Army moved to London and Charles was taken to Hampton Court Palace, where he quickly settled into the royal apartments.

Whilst the Army and Parliament were in dispute, the King, with the assistance of some loyal followers, managed to escape from Hampton Court.

Cromwell reported to the Speaker of the House of Commons that,

"His Majesty was expected at supper, when the Commissioners and Colonel Whalley missed him. Upon which they entered the room; they found his Majesty had left his cloak behind him in the gallery in the private way. He passed, by the backstairs and vault, towards the waterside."

11. Hampton Court Palace.

Charles left behind a letter explaining his action and casting some doubts on the sincerity of the Army leaders. He explained that he had "...just cause to free myself from the hands of those who change their principles." He also complained,

"How many times have I desired, pressed to be heard, and yet no ear given to me? And can any reasonable man think, that according to the ordinary course of affairs there can be a settled peace without it or that God will bless those who refuse to hear their own King? Surely no."

Sir John Berkeley, who had been in attendance on the King at Hampton Court explained that the King left, "...for feare of being murder'd privatly." Charles was well aware of the dangers of imprisonment and the threat of his being murdered secretly was real and a matter of concern to the King's loyal subjects. His opponents were, however, men of principle. They believed that God was on their side and were determined that whatever actions were to be taken should be public and beyond reproach. With this attitude they were anxious to protect the King's person from any unlawful attack.

One letter from the King left behind at Hampton Court written to Colonel Whaley, one of his guardians, thanked him for his kindness and courtesy and asked him to ensure that, "...my household and moveables of all sorts, which I leave behind me in this House; that they be neither spoiled nor embezzled." He also mentioned four specific paintings hung at Hampton Court, which had been loaned to him. He described each painting in detail and their exact locations and asked for them to be returned to their rightful owners.

In a postscript to this note, the King added,

"...I confess I am loath to be made a close prisoner under pretence of securing my life. I had almost forgot to desire you to send the black grew [greyhound] bitch to the Duke of Richmond."

It is interesting that at such a time the King should concern himself with such apparently trivial matters.

On leaving Hampton Court, the King appeared to have no clear destination in mind. The West Country was considered as was flight abroad. The small group headed towards Long Sutton in Hampshire, but in the dark and stormy night they missed their way and did not arrive there until daybreak. An Inn they had intended to use was found to be occupied by one of the Committees appointed by Parliament and after changing their horses, they headed towards Southampton. Eventually, and hastened by the prospect of recapture if he stayed too long in one place, the King decided on the Isle of Wight, where it was thought he would be well received by loyal subjects. The King was familiar with the island and had made several visits there in more peaceful times. Sir John Berkeley and Colonel John Ashburnham went ahead of the King to make the necessary arrangements.

The Governor of the island was Colonel Robert Hammond, who it was believed would be sympathetic to the King.

When, however, Hammond was told by Berkeley that the King was approaching the island, his response was,

"...you have undone me by bringing the King into the Island, if at least you have brought him, and if you have not, pray let him not come; for what between my duty to His Majesty and by Gratitude for this fresh obligation of Confidence, and my observing my Trust to the Army, I shall be confounded."

Berkeley and Ashburnham told Hammond that the King had fled for his life and Hammond then agreed, as a person of honour, to offer his protection.

It was asserted at the time that the King's escape from Hampton Court had been planned by Cromwell and that it was he who appointed Hammond to his position on the Isle of Wight. This story was based on rumours, but may have had some element of truth. Hammond's appointment was swift and unexpected and he arrived on the Isle of Wight only a few days before the King, at a "...season when there was no visible occasion to draw him hither."

Newsletters at the time commented that his timely arrival on the island was, "...as if by instinct he had foreseen his Majesties coming."

Although in effect a prisoner, once on the island, everything possible was done to make the King comfortable and he was lodged at Carisbrooke Castle. Charles was to enjoy a good relationship with Hammond. "I am daily more and more satisfied with the Governor," the King wrote.

12. Charles I and Colonel Hammond, the Governor of Carisbrooke Castle.

Carisbrooke Castle has Saxon origins and has been added to and enlarged over the centuries. A Norman Keep dominates the site and the fourteenth century walls enclose a large area which contains many later buildings, several of which are today in ruins. Charles was accommodated in domestic apartments adjacent to the original Great Hall of the castle, which faces towards the main castle entrance. These buildings still survive, although they were heavily restored in 1856, following two centuries of neglect.

Parliament allowed some of the King's former servants to join him from Hampton Court, and in November some choice pieces of furniture were moved from the King's private apartments at Hampton Court to the island.

The King was not close-confined and within a day or so of his arrival on the island he was out hunting deer and hawking. He was free to travel the island, and did so. In December his royal coach was shipped to him, which must have been a great curiosity as there were few coaches of any type on the island, let alone royal ones. Charles now "...went abroad to view the Island and to observe the several accommodations of it." An anonymous contemporary letter describes the King's activities whilst a prisoner at Carisbroke.

> " His Majestie, after morning prayer, takes usually before dinner some 6 or 8 circuits of the Castle wall and the like in the afternoon, if fair; much time spent every day in private. He speaks most to us at dinner, asks newes, particularly concerning Ireland, Scotland, the City of London and the Army... His Majesty is merry as formerly. All quiet and faire twixt his Majesty and Col. Hammond the Governor... When messengers came from London the King asks how his children do and seems to desire to know what the Parliament will do."

Charles spent much of his time reading and writing. One way of relieving the boredom was for him to play a game of bowls on a bowling green which had been constructed specifically for him on the orders of Hammond. The new green was built between the outer and inner walls of the castle and a game of bowls became part of the daily routine whenever the weather allowed. The King was,

> "...very well pleased with the bowling alley, which is now finished and the bowls being come his Majesty was very merry to play with Colonell Hammond."

In April the King remarked how hot the bowling green would be in the summer months; clearly he expected to remain at Carisbroke for some time.

Many of the islanders evidently were allowed access to the King. One report in April commented that the King, "...touched above 20 for the cure of the Evill as he came down to dinner." It was believed that the King's touch could cure certain diseases. In May it was reported that,

> "...many come to be cured of the Evill, but... the heat of the weather coming on there will be a stop, to prevent the danger of his Majesties person."

Both Parliament and the Army suspected that the King's flight to the Isle of Wight had been intended as a means of escaping abroad more easily. In December, news reached London that the Queen was in Jersey, and that Hammond had been forced to flee from the Isle of Wight by the inhabitants of the island who had risen to help the King. It was only a rumour, but the result was that Hammond began to keep tighter control over the King and his freedom was restricted.

Charles, however, had not been idle and had made the most of his freedom on the island. He had managed to send letters to the Scots, with whom he had reopened negotiations. Letters were smuggled to and from the castle, with the assistance of many of the King's servants, including the Assistant Laundress, who was able to hide letters to the King under his carpets and collect letters from him with his laundry. These letters were, however, intercepted by the Army and once read, resealed and forwarded. The replies were also intercepted, all unbeknown to the King.

On Boxing Day in 1647, Charles made an agreement with the Scots to establish Presbyterianism in England for three years, in return for their military help,

> "...for preservation and establishment of religion, for defence of His Majesty's person and authority and restoring him to his government, to the just rights of the Crown and his full revenues."

When Parliament heard of this agreement, all negotiations with the King were stopped and the King was placed under close guard.

At almost the same time, a minor public disturbance caused by Royalist supporters on the island put the military on full alert and Hammond set about to improve the security of the island, even putting the castle in a state of readiness for any attack on its defences.

Rumours of escape plans began to circulate and Hammond prevented the King from seeing his usual visitors, who had had until this time almost unrestricted access.

Parliament ordered a purge of the royal servants in February. The number was reduced significantly to thirty and those who had been suspected of being involved in the smuggling of letters were removed. The grooms of the bedchamber, the servants closest to the King, were also dismissed and Charles had grudgingly to accept two new grooms, Thomas Herbert and James Harrington, both appointed by Parliament. Even the King's barber was dismissed, and as Charles refused to submit to a razor wielded by a Parliamentarian, his hair and beard grew so long that he was often described as looking like a hermit.

Charles still managed to communicate with supporters outside with the help of a few of his remaining servants, and an escape plan was prepared. It was noticed that the guard did not patrol the inner courtyard of the castle and that if Charles could climb through his window, it would be relatively easy to smuggle him out of the castle over the low defences. Loyal supporters would be ready with horses to take the King to a waiting boat, for any destination he should choose.

The day for the escape was fixed for Monday, 20th March, 1648. As darkness fell, everyone was in position and the King lowered a rope, which had previously been hidden in his chamber, from his window. The King did not get very far, for it soon became apparent that the window was too small for him to climb through. The window was fitted with a central iron bar which had already been the subject of much debate. The King maintained that he had previously tried and succeeded in getting his head through the gap which had been enough to convince him that there was room for him to climb through. He had been against any tampering with the bar which might have been discovered before he was able to make good his escape. Charles struggled back into his chamber and then lit a candle in the window to indicate that the escape plan had to be abandoned.

Not long after Charles's failed escape attempt, news reached him that his second son, James, Duke of York, had been freed from St. James's Palace in a daring rescue, which had included disguising the Duke as a woman. The news that the Duke had escaped to Holland pleased the King, but it underlined the futility of his own position.

At the end of March, Hammond learned about the failed escape attempt and also of rumours that another attempt was being planned.

Charles was indeed plotting another escape and on this occasion he was determined not to be thwarted by too small an opening in the window. There was copious correspondence to and from the King on the best methods of removing window bars without being discovered; most of it was intercepted. The new plan was, broadly speaking, very similar to the first, but included the idea of providing a disguise for the King to enable him to make his escape from the castle under the very noses of the guards. At the end of April, the escape plan received a slight setback as the King was moved to new rooms in the castle. Luckily, one of these rooms too had a window from which an escape was possible, although this one was also fitted with a metal bar which needed to be removed. One of the King's

13. The window through which Charles I tried to escape in March 1648. The King's window is the lowest of the set of four beneath the high gable. After a drawing of 1798. In 1856 the windows were remodelled.

servants began filing through the bar and the cut was disguised with wax or clay, "...soe that it cannot be perceiv'd." Once again supporters arranged to meet the King with horses and a boat was to be in readiness.

It was 29th May when the plan was ready to be put into action, although by this time Hammond was aware of it and was prepared.

The escape failed. The exact reasons why are not known. One account states that the rope snapped, another that the King, "...discern'd more persons to stand thereabout than used to do so, and so shut the window and went back to bed." The most likely version is that some of the King's supporters were inside the castle and that, in the dark, they mistook one of the guards for a friend and so gave the game away. The Royalists fled from the castle guards in a hail of badly-aimed musket balls and managed to hide in woods overnight before making good their escape the next morning.

Hammond entered the King's bedchamber and found "...the window-bar ....to be cut in two in the middle." Charles was left, "...very much troubled and discontent," having failed in this escape attempt, this time through no apparent fault of his own.

Meanwhile the agreement Charles had made with the Scots encouraged many Royalists to orchestrate several small risings around the country, which were quickly put down by the Army. Lord Fairfax put down revolts in Kent and Essex and Oliver Cromwell a revolt in Wales. In the summer of 1648 the Scottish army, under the command of the Duke of Hamilton, marched into England, reaching as far south as Preston where it was defeated by Cromwell.

Parliament reopened talks with the King once again, a move which was to anger the Army Commanders who had become tired of the seemingly endless and fruitless series of negotiations. The opinion of the Army was voiced in the *Remonstrance of the Army* of 1648 which demanded of Parliament that the King be brought to trial, "...for the treason, blood and mischief he is therein guilty of."

Charles realised the significance of this new development and the implications of the *Remonstrance* to him, but wrote of it calmly to the Prince of Wales. "This may be the last time we may speak to you or the world publicly. We are sensible into what hands we are fallen."

Talks between Parliament and the Army came to nothing as once again neither would make any concessions. In the November of 1648, the Commissioners of Parliament went to Carisbrooke to negotiate with the King. The agreement allowed the King some freedom, but he had to agree that he would not try to escape again. During the negotiations a dog belonging to the King, "...which his majesty calls Rogue," and a dog (called Titus) belonging to one of the Commissioners, the Earl of Middlesex,

"...snarled and fought together in the room, whereupon causing some interruption, his Majesty said, 'These dogs disturb us, but none but dogs will hinder the treaty.'"

Having reached some agreement, the King obviously assumed that his position had improved and he finally trimmed his "hermit beard" and commented that with this he "...had begun the Reformation."

Charles celebrated his forty-eighth birthday on Sunday 19th November on the Isle of Wight. He had begun to look his age; his cheeks had become sunken and he had deep pouches beneath his eyes. His hair and beard had turned very grey.

14. The King imprisoned in Carisbrooke Castle.

Several mementos of the King remain at Carisbrooke Castle. On one of his last days there the King was on the bowling green and was amused to see the nine year old son of Howe, the master gunner of the Castle, marching up and down with a toy wooden sword.

"What are you going to do with that terrible weapon?" he asked.

"Please your Majesty," was the reply, "I am going to defend you with it from all your enemies."

The King patted the boy on the head and gave him his blessing, saying, "Well my little friend, I am just going away from here, and I do not expect that I shall ever return. I would like to give you something in order that you may always remember me." The gift was a ruby ring.

The ring remains at Carisbrooke today, along with a head of a walking stick, which the King gave to Howe, the master gunner, and a linen cap.

Another memento which dates to this time is now in Dunham Massey House in Cheshire. It is a blue silk ribbon worn around the neck of the King, to which was attached the *George* of the Order of the Garter.

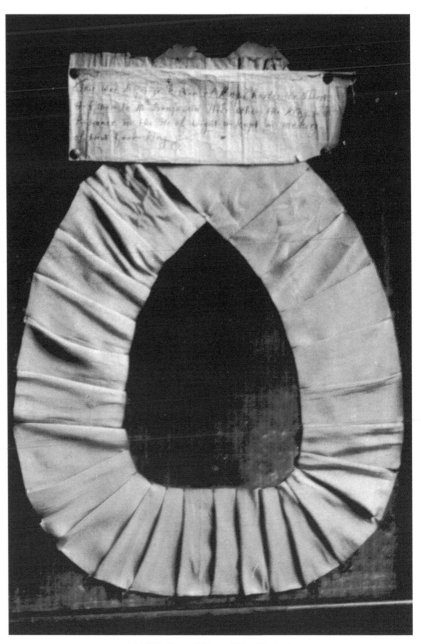

15. The Garter Ribbon of King Charles I

Mounted behind glass, a handwritten note states:

> "This was a George ribbon of King Charles I and given to Mr Benjamin Hide when the king was a prisoner in the Isle of Wight and kept in memory of that good king."

Another hand-written note, mounted behind a panel on the reverse of the frame states:

> "Mr Benjamin Hide....was a merchant trading with his own ships in the Mediterranean. He was very intimate with his brother-in-law Sir Edward Ford, who exerted himself much in the King's behalf; and - though not mentioned in the History of the time, it is thought that the kindly office which brought Mr Hide under the King's notice was an unsuccessful endeavour to scheme a safe passage for His Majesty in one of his ships."

At the end of November, Charles was moved by the Army from Carisbrooke to Hurst Castle, a small, but secure place on the mainland near the Solent. The move was initiated following the disclosure of a possible threat to the King's life. The King now found himself closely confined in the desolate little fort, castle being perhaps too grand a name, standing on the end of a causeway, two or three miles in length.

The accommodation was dismal and the castle was constantly surrounded by winter fogs and mists which meant that the small rooms needed to be lit by candles even at midday. The King's only exercise was to walk along the shingle of the causeway at low tide.

Charles had time to reflect on his possible fate, but was sure that he could not be brought to trial by any legal means. He wrote on the *Remonstrance of the Army,*

> "...by the letter of the law, all persons charged to offend against the law ought to be tried by their peers or equals. What is the law if the person questioned is without peer?"

Parliament rejected the *Remonstrance* and proposed to continue negotiations with the King. The Army, however, had other ideas and acted swiftly, moving on London and occupying Westminster. The night of 5th December was spent preparing lists of members of the House of Commons who were known to be supporters of the Army. That same night, the City Trained Bands, citizen volunteers who had the task of patrolling the approaches to Parliament, were surprised to find their role usurped by the

Army, who were guarding every approach to Parliament.

On 6th December, Colonel Pride positioned himself and a body of troops at the top of the stairs leading into Parliament House and enquired the name of each member as he arrived. Each name was checked on the list and only the known supporters of the Army were allowed to enter. Fairfax and his officers issued a declaration in which they stated that they had liberated Parliament, which would enable it to carry out its duties without the "...interruptions, diversion and depravations" of self-interested colleagues.

Cromwell arrived in London the day after "Pride's Purge" of Parliament, and whilst he declared that he had known nothing of the plan, he approved of the result. The Army was now in complete control of Parliament and the capital.

Cromwell, whose views had been unspoken, at least in public, before he came to London, agreed that the King should be put on trial, but had not yet voiced the idea of a death sentence being the likely outcome, rather than deposition or exile. Before Christmas, however, he had made up his mind and commented on Charles's actions. "If any man had deliberately designed such a thing, he would be the greatest traitor in the world." The inevitable penalty for a convicted traitor was death.

By this time the King had been moved yet again, this time under strong guard to Windsor Castle. He left Hurst Castle on 19th December and rode on horseback to Winchester, where he was greeted with the customary homage by the Mayor and Corporation (who were afterwards rebuked for their courtesy). At Windsor he was met by Colonel Harrison who escorted the King to Windsor, where he arrived on 23rd December. Some of the inhabitants of Windsor rioted at the way the King was being treated by the Army and some civilians were killed by the soldiers.

Charles now knew that the trial was inevitable. His views, published in the broadsheets of the time, were that he considered himself blameless, but that he was resigned to God's will.

Whilst the much-reduced, Army-controlled Parliament (now known as the "Rump" following Pride's Purge of Members) was still considering bringing the King to trial, speculation in the country was rife and included reports that there would be no trial and certainly no execution but that Parliament would "work him by terror to renounce the regal dignity." Perhaps the King would even be restored to his throne, but with severely reduced powers.

The idea of the King's being executed was to most people, at this time, unthinkable.

At Windsor the King enjoyed the Christmas celebrations. He dined as usual, under a canopy in full state, waited upon by his servants. Tailors

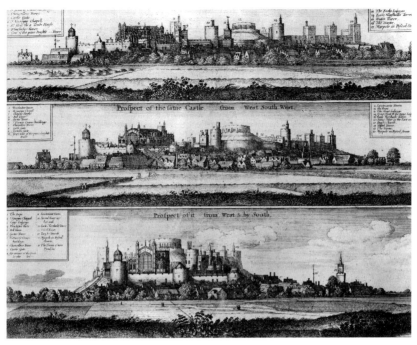

16. Contemporary views of Windsor Castle.

from London had provided him with a quantity of new clothes. The celebrations, to the King's disappointment, did not include the traditional "minc'd pye", nor the predecessor of plum pudding, "plum porridge".

There were no chaplains in attendance, so the King, dressed in his finest clothes, read the appointed service himself from the Book of Common Prayer to those gathered.

The King's formal meals were the occasion for visitors to be allowed admittance into his presence. This practice was soon stopped and the King's personal attendants were reduced in number to six. Charles decided he would, forthwith, have his meals privately in his own chamber and would choose from a daily menu prepared for him. Much of his time was spent in private, where he passed the time reading the Bible and plays by Shakespeare and Ben Jonson.

Parliament, having finally decided on its course of action, passed an act to create a special High Court of Justice for the trial of the King.

A Royalist, writing just before the trial stated that,

"...never was such damnable doctrine vented before in the world for the persons of sovereign princes have ever been held sacred...although in many kingdoms they have been regulated by force of arms and sometimes...deposed and afterwards privately murdered, yet in no history can we find a parallel for this...to bring their sovereign lord to public trial and execution, it being contrary to the law of nature, the custom of nations and the sacred scriptures...What court shall their king be tried in? Who shall be his peers? Who shall give sentence? What eyes dare be so impious to behold the execution?"

IV TRIAL

Parliament had now decided that the King must be brought to trial and they determined to accuse him of the crime of treason, defined as "treachery towards one's country".

An Ordinance to establish a court to try the King was drawn up by the House of Commons.

> "Whereas it is notorious that Charles Stuart, the now King of England...hath had a wicked design totally to subvert the ancient and fundamental laws and liberties of this Nation and in their place to introduce an arbitrary and tyrannical government, and that, besides all other evil ways and means to bring this design to pass, he hath prosecuted it with fire and sword, levied and maintained a cruel war in the land against Parliament and Kingdom whereby the country hath been miserably wasted, the public Treasure exhausted, trade decayed, thousands of people murdered and infinite other mischiefs committed...Whereas also the Parliament, well hoping that the restraint and imprisonment of his person, after it had pleased God to deliver him into their hands, would have quietened the distempers of the Kingdom, did forbear to proceed judicially against him, but found by sad experience, that such their remissness served only to encourage him and his complices in the continuance of their evil practices and in raising new commotions, rebellions and invasions..."

The Ordinance was then passed to the House of Lords for their approval, as was the usual procedure. The House of Lords was not, however, in session. The Lords was greatly reduced in numbers and none of the Royalist Peers had been in attendance for many years. On New Year's Day 1649, those Peers remaining had declared themselves a holiday and the Ordinance "touching the King would have to wait."

The next day, the Lords assembled, all seven of them. None present were supporters of the King, but all were swift to uphold the laws of the land against any action by the House of Commons.

Ironically, the Earl of Manchester, who at the outset of the Civil Wars had been one of the chief opponents of the King, now declared that the

King alone had the power to call or dissolve Parliament and that it was, therefore, absurd to accuse him of treason against a body over which he had the ultimate authority.

The Earl of Northumberland also doubted if the majority of the people of England could state with any certainty that it was the King who had started the War and not Parliament. Without proving that point, the King could never be accused of treason. The Earl of Denbeigh stated that he would rather be torn in pieces than have any part in so infamous a business. The Lords unanimously rejected the Ordinance.

The House of Commons' response was to assert their right to proceed without further reference to the Lords. The names of any Peers on the list of the King's judges were removed from the Ordinance, which was hurriedly given a first and second reading in one session and passed with only a narrow majority on 6th January. This, and the fact that the House of Lords was excluded, makes it easy to understand later claims that the House of Commons alone could not set up a High Court of Justice, nor that it actually represented the people of England.

At ten o'clock on Tuesday 9th January the Sergeant at Arms, Edward Dendy, rode into Westminster Hall, attended by six trumpeters and two troops of horse. There, in the middle of the Hall, where the Court of Chancery was in full session, he interrupted the proceedings and formally proclaimed that Charles Stuart, King of England was to be put on trial. Members of the Commons present were so pleased by the performance they ordered him to repeat it at Cheapside and the Old Exchange, which he did later the same morning.

Parliament ordained that,

> "Thomas, Lord Fairfax, Oliver Cromwell, Henry Ireton [and others] shall be and are hereby appointed and required to be Commissioners and Judges for the hearing, trying and judging of the said Charles Stuart."

In total, one hundred and fifty Commissioners were appointed to sit as judges in the special High Court. The list included the chief officers of the Army, Aldermen and citizens of the City of London and some country gentlemen; all of them were supporters of Parliament.

John Bradshaw, a barrister, whose family home was in Cheshire, was appointed as President of the Court. Clarendon was later to state that Bradshaw was, "...not much known" in the courts of the time and went on to describe him as being of "...great insolence and ambition."

From 8th January, the Commissioners for the King's Trial began meeting in the Painted Chamber in the Palace of Westminster. Many of those present doubted their right to try the King, but Cromwell expressed his views forcibly, "I tell you we will cut off his head with the Crown upon it!"

The authority of the Court was important and up until the day before the trial was due to start, the Commissioners appear not to have satisfied themselves on this point. Whilst this matter was still being discussed, Charles arrived at Westminster and could be seen entering the garden under escort. Cromwell said to the other Commissioners present,

"I desire you to let us resolve here what answer we shall give the King when he comes before us, for the first question he will ask us will be by what authority and Commission do we try him."

Henry Marten provided the answer which met with the approval of the Commissioners present, "In the name of the Commons in Parliament assembled and all the good people of England."

The Commissioners discussed how the trial should be conducted and agreed that,

"...in case the prisoner shall in language or carriage towards the court be insolent, outrageous or contemptuous, that it be left to the lord president to reprehend him therefore and admonish him of his duty or to command the taking away of the prisoner and, if he sees cause, to withdraw or adjourn the court. But as to the prisoner's putting off his hat, the court will not insist upon it for this day, and that if the king desire time to answer, the lord president is to give him time."

Whilst the charge was being drafted, a group of Commissioners went to inspect Westminster Hall, which was to be the setting for the trial. A major trial there must have involved considerable disturbance, as the Hall was the general meeting place and clearing house for justice and the home of a number of courts, which were roughly partitioned off from each other in the vast open space. In addition to the courts there were many traders' stalls set around the walls of the Hall and there needed to be a great deal of demolition and refitting before the trial of the King could be "...performed in a solemn manner."

It was considered essential that the trial be held in public, but also that it be secure. The Commissioners recommended that the trial be heard at the south end of the Hall, where sufficient space could be cleared. The rest of the Hall would provide room for the public.

For most public trials, it would have been usual for the prisoner to be seated at the centre of the court, surrounded by the public. This

17. The exterior of Westminster Hall.

would also have meant that any prisoner would have to walk through the public to reach his allotted place in the Court. The decision to hold the trial at one end of the Hall was taken to protect the King from any possible attack from members of the public. It meant that he would not have to be taken through the public area, but could be taken directly into the Hall under cover from the security of adjoining buildings.

In effect, the setting gave only the appearance of a public trial, as the majority of the those present would have been able to see and hear little.

It was decided to erect some public galleries which would directly overlook the trial; the security risk was considered slight as any spectators in the galleries would have to enter and leave the Hall from a secure area. All these precautions were put into place to protect the King, but Bradshaw, the President of the Court, was concerned for his own safety and took the precaution of wearing a hat lined with steel plates when the Court was in session.

As Westminster Hall was being cleared and the galleries and benches assembled, orders were sent to the Tower Armouries for additional halberds for the guards. Formal black gowns had been ordered for the officials of the Court.

On Friday 19th January, 1649, Charles was brought by coach from Windsor Castle to London, where he was lodged initially at St. James's Palace. Few people knew he was being moved and his carriage, drawn by six horses, was taken right into the heart of the Castle to collect him. He

18. The steel reinforced hat worn at the trial by Bradshaw. Ashmolean Museum, Oxford.

was no longer given all the usual respects due to his position as Sovereign and Clarendon wrote that,

> "...from the time of the King's being come to St. James's....his Majesty was treated with more rudeness and barbarity than he had ever been before. No man was suffered to see or speak to him, but the soldiers who were his guard, some of whom sat up always in his bedchamber and drank and took tobacco...nor was he suffered to go into any other room, either to say his prayers or to receive the ordinary benefits of nature, but was obliged to do both in their presence and before them."

The next day the Army presented an *Agreement of the People* to Parliament. It was now evident, if it had not been so before, that the Army was ready to impose a death penalty on the King.

> "It is agreed that whosoever shall, by force of arms render up, or give, or take away the foundations of common right, liberty and safety...he shall forthwith lose the benefit and protection of the laws and shall be punishable with death as an enemy and traitor to the Nation."

The King was to be lodged for the duration of the trial at Sir Robert Cotton's house, which was within the Palace of Westminster, and, therefore, quite secure.

19. The interior of Westminster Hall.

Charles knew the trial was about to commence, but he had not seen the Act of Parliament which had established the court and he had no idea who his judges were to be. When told of the trial, Charles received the news with his usual calm. He is reported as having spoke little on the subject, other than to say that he considered that no one had any authority to try him. He would recognise no court but God, would answer no charge the court might put to him and would, if necessary, die a martyr.

The trial was at last ready to begin. By this time it would appear that all those who were set to try the King had already concluded that he was guilty and should receive the death sentence. On the afternoon of Saturday 20th January, just after two o'clock, the trial opened.

The Commissioners entered the Hall, proceeded by twenty halberdiers and officers carrying the Sword of State and Mace, and followed by more guards. They took their places on tiered benches, covered in red material, erected beneath the great south window of the Hall.

Bradshaw was seated in the middle of the front row on a raised platform. He had a reading desk and a scarlet cushion set in front of him. On either side of Bradshaw sat a Commissioner who had been chosen to assist him on points of law. All three wore black barrister's gowns. The other Commissioners wore suitably sober attire.

The guards took up their positions around the edges of the Court and beneath the public galleries around the area.

An armchair, covered in red velvet, had been placed in position for

20. A contemporary view of the trial in Westminster Hall. Ashmolean Museum, Oxford.

21. The chair and footstool, commonly identified as that used by Charles I at the trial.

the King, facing the Commissioners. A small side-table equipped with pen-and-ink stood ready for the King's use if required.

A chair, formerly in the possession of Bishop Juxon and now on display in the Victoria and Albert Museum, has, for over three hundred years, been associated with Charles I. Tradition has it that it was the chair used by the King at the trial and that it was claimed by Juxon as a perquisite after the execution. It is certainly of a design typical of the period, but recent research has cast some doubt on its use at the trial. It may date to the Restoration of Charles II in 1660, when Juxon was made Archbishop of Canterbury and had a "Chaire of State and foot stoole" made for him.

A proclamation for silence was made by the Crier to the assembled court.

"Ho Yes! Ho Yes! Ho Yes! All manner of persons that have anything to do in this Court, come in and give your attendance.

Ho Yes! Every man keep silence upon pain of imprisonment and hear the commissions of this Court read, which is authorised by and Act of the Commons of England in Parliament assembled."

The Act constituting the Court was read, with each Commissioner answering to his name by standing up when it was called out. It was then discovered that less than half of the total number of Commissioners had chosen to be there - only sixty-eight in all. Even Lord Fairfax was absent. A voice from the gallery, believed to be that of Lady Fairfax, was heard to say that, "...he had more wit than to be there."

When the roll-call ended, the Serjeant at Arms took up the Mace, intending to fetch the King into the Court, but he was ordered to replace it. Twelve men with partisans were sent instead.

The King was preceded and followed into the Hall by soldiers. He walked quickly, looking neither right nor left and seated himself in the chair made ready for him. His face showed no flicker of recognition of anyone present nor any curiosity. He was dressed in black. Around his neck he wore the blue ribbon and jewelled *George* of the Order of the Garter and the star of the Garter was embroidered on his black cloak. He wore a tall black hat over his greying hair. The only people in the Court who would have been able to see his face clearly would have been the Commissioners and the public in the raised galleries. The King was seated with his back to the main public area and the wooden partition across the Hall, separating the court from the public. This would have meant that all that most of the public would have seen of him was the top of his hat.

Bradshaw opened the proceedings.

"Charles Stuart, King of England, the Commons of England assembled in Parliament being deeply sensible of the calamities that have been brought upon this Nation, which is fixed upon you as the principal author of it, have resolved to make inquisition for blood; and according to that debt and duty they owe to justice, to God, the Kingdom and themselves, and according to the fundamental power that rests in themselves, they have resolved to bring you to trial and judgement; and for that purpose have constituted the High Court of Justice, before which you are brought and you are to hear your charge upon which the Court will proceed."

The charge was read by John Cook, who entered into this role with obvious enthusiasm. The charge, which was lengthy, accused the King of ruling as a tyrant and waging war against the Parliament and people. It listed many of the battles and skirmishes of the Civil Wars which had,

"...caused and procured many thousands of the free people of this nation to be slain." It continued by stating that,

> "All which wicked designs, warrs and evill practices of him the said Charles Stuart have bin and are carried on for the advancement and upholding of a personal interest of will, power and pretended prerogative to himself and his family, against the publick interest, common right, liberty, justice and peace of the people of this nation... The said Charles Stuart hath been, and is the occasioner, author, and continuer of the said unnatural cruel and bloody wars; and therein guilty of all the treasons, murders, rapines, burnings, spoils, desolations, damages and mischiefs to this Nation, acted and committed in the said wars, or occasioned thereby."

The final section of the charge stated that the Court,

> "...doth for the said treasons and crimes, on behalf of the said people of England, impeach the said Charles Stuart as a tyrant, traytor, murtherer and a public and implacable enemy to the commonwealth of England, and pray that the said Charles Stuart, King of England, may be put to answere all and every the premises and that such proceedings, examinations, trials, sentences and judgements may be thereupon had, as shall be agreeable to justice."

During the lengthy reading of the charge, Charles tried to interrupt Cook, who was standing near him, by tapping him with a silver headed cane. As the King did so the head of the cane fell to the floor. For a moment Charles waited, until he realised that there was no one who would retrieve it for him, when he then stooped to retrieve it himself, placing the head in his pocket. This event was seen as being significant and, if nothing else, was to remind Charles that he was indeed on his own.

Whilst the charge was being read, the King looked up at the galleries and scanned the faces of the Commissioners before him. He also turned to look at the crowds seated behind him in the Hall. His face still showed no emotion.

On hearing the final words of the charge, Charles laughed in the face of the Court.

After the charge had been read, Lady Anna De Lille, who was in the gallery, called out that it was not the King's subjects who made the charge against him, but only "traitors and rebels". She is reported to have been seized and branded by hot irons on her shoulder and her head, to the horror of the King. Many years after the event, it was recorded that, "His Majesty then seeing her flesh smoake and her haire all of a fire for him by their hot irons, much commiserated her, and wished he could have been able to have requited her."

Exactly why, "hot brands" should be so readily available in the court, must be a matter of conjecture. It was a cold January and there may have been some form of heating installed in the Hall, or it is possible that they were used for the melting of sealing wax.

After this unusual interlude, Bradshaw requested an answer to the charge from the King.

Charles had never been a good speaker in public and still suffered from a slight speech impediment, but his reply was loud and clear.

"I would know by what power I am called hither," he began,

"I would know by what authority, I mean *lawful*....There are many unlawful authorities in the world, thieves and robbers by the highway... Remember I am your King, your *Lawful* King....I have a trust committed to me by God by old and lawful descent. I will not betray it to answer a new and unlawful authority. Therefore resolve me that and you shall hear more of me."

Bradshaw replied that he should answer "...in the name of the people of England," and added, "of which you are elected King." Bradshaw had made a mistake here and Charles was quick to respond.

"England was never an elective Kingdom, but an hereditary Kingdom for near these thousand years, therefore let me know by what authority I am called hither: I do stand more for the liberty of my people than any one that is seated here as a judges. Therefore show me by what lawful authority I am seated here and I will answer it. Otherwise I will not betray the liberties of my people."

Bradhaw was not able to reply to this and he covered his confusion by trying unsuccessfully to rebuke the King for his attitude towards the Court. Charles continued to assert the illegality of the Court, as Cromwell had known he would, and was not deflected by the formal response to this question which the Commissioners had prepared earlier.

The King continued,

"...I do not come here as submitting to the court. I will stand as much for the privilege of the House of Commons as any man whatsoever. I see no House of Lords that may constitute a Parliament for this your bringing back your King to your Parliament... Therefore, let me see a legal authority, I say a legal authority, warranted either by the Word of God, by Scripture, or warranted by the ancient laws and constitutions of this realm and I will answer."

Bradshaw decided there was no alternative but to bring the day's proceedings to a close and ordered the King to be removed.

Charles continued to put forward his views and was eventually led away, to the orchestrated cries from the soldiers present of "Justice! Justice!" whilst others shouted "God Save the King!"

The day's proceedings ended with another proclamation by the crier.

"Ho Yes! Ho Yes! Ho Yes! All manner or persons that have any thing more to do at this court, ye are to depart at this time. And this court doth adjourn itself until Monday morning next, at 9 of the clocke to meet in the Painted Chamber and from thence hither again."

Back at the King's lodgings, two soldiers were ordered to keep watch in his bedchamber, whereupon Charles refused flatly to go to his bed. Other attempts were made to break down the King's spirit by attempting to conduct his devotions for him on the Sunday, but he refused to hear the person sent. Having not slept on the Saturday night, the King did go to bed on the Sunday.

On the Sunday the Court did not sit. Charles took the opportunity to prepare a statement, in which he continued to assert that the Court could never be lawful and in which he rejected the view that it represented the feelings of the English people. Charles hoped to read this statement at the next sitting of the Court, but, in the event, he was not allowed to do so.

The Court reconvened on Monday the 22nd. The crier again opened the proceedings and the list of Commissioners was read aloud. The crier made one more proclamation to the people assembled in the Court.

"My lord President and this high court doth strictly charge and command all persons to keep silence during the sitting of this court, and the Captain of the guards is to apprehend all such persons as shall make any disturbance."

This was to prevent any further outbursts from any supporters of the King who might be present.

The King was sent for; this time the Serjeant at Arms, bearing the Mace, performed the duty.

Cook was slow to open the proceedings and Charles, who was keen to begin, once again prodded him with his cane. Cook announced that the charge of High Treason had already been read to the prisoner, who had not seen fit to respond, but had decided instead to dispute the power and authority of the Court. Cook went on to say that if the King should continue to refuse to give an answer, to either deny or admit to the charge, that "...the matter of the charge may be taken *pro confesso*, and the court may proceed according to justice."

Bradhaw added his voice to this threat to the King.

Charles interrupted to set out once again the weakness of the Court's position, a matter to which he had given some thought when the Court was in recess on the Sunday.

"For if the power without law may make laws, may alter the fundamental laws of the Kingdom, I do not know what subject be in England, that can be sure of his life, or anything he calls his own."

Bradshaw demanded an answer to the charge from the King, who still challenged the authority of the Court. Bradhaw had to interrupt.

"Sir, you are not to dispute our authority, you are told of it again by the Court. Sir, it will be taken notice of that you stand in contempt of the Court, and your contempt will be recorded accordingly."

The new charge of Contempt of Court was nothing compared to the seriousness of the main charges facing the King and, not surprisingly, Charles paid little attention to it, but continued and asserted that any accused person had the right to show why he questioned the legality of a court. He had already stated that he was, "...no lawyer professed, but I know as much law as any gentleman in England."

Charles questioned the assertion that the House of Commons alone was a Court.

Bradshaw told the King,

"I must let you know the mind of this court. They overrule your demurrer. You dispute their authority. You are called here to account by the authority of this Court. We sit here by the authority of the Commons of England, and that authority has called your ancestors (the greatest of them) to account."

"I deny that," said the King. "Show me one precedent."

Bradshaw could not and told the King that, "the matter was not to be debated by you, neither will the court permit you to do it..."

Charles answered that whilst Parliament, comprising the two Houses, of Commons *and* Lords, was a Court, the House of Commons *alone* was not. "I say Sir, by your favour, that the Commons of England was never a Court of Judicature, I would know how they came to be so."

Bradshaw in desperation again demanded that the King answer the charge. When Charles refused to do so, Bradshaw threatened that the next sitting of the Court would be the last and ordered him to be removed.

Charles, however, refused to go easily and said,

> "...I will answer the same as soon as I know by what authority you do this....I do require that I may give in my reasons why I do not answer, and give me time for that."

Bradshaw retorted that "It is not for prisoners to require."

"Sir," said the King, "I am not an ordinary prisoner." Charles still made no effort to rise and leave the Court as ordered, nor did the Guard attempt to force him to leave. "Remember," he said, "that the King is not suffered to give his reasons for the liberty and freedom of all his subjects."

Bradshaw replied, "How great a friend you have been to the laws and liberties of the People, let all England and the world judge!"

Charles replied, but for the first time at the trial his speech was hesitant.

> "Sir, under favour, it was the liberty, freedom and laws of the subject, that I ever took - defended myself with arms. I never took up arms against the people, but for the laws."

The sitting of the Court ended with the proceedings again having stagnated. Charles was still making his protests as the guards took him from the Hall, once again to the cries from the soldiers of "Justice!"

One soldier said "God bless you sir" as the King passed. Charles thanked him, and when the soldier was struck by one of his officers for making such a remark, Charles commented that, "the punishment exceeds the offence."

In his room in Cotton House, the King remarked to those present that he only recognised about eight of the faces of the Commissioners who were to judge him and he enquired about the composition of the Court. He wanted to know who sat in judgement against him.

On the third day, Tuesday 23rd January, the proceedings of the Court began with the usual proclamations and roll-call of Commissioners, before the King was brought into Westminster Hall.

22. Charles I at the trial. Portrait by or after Edward Bower.

Cook began by insisting that the King was guilty and requesting that "...speedy judgement be pronounced against the prisoner at the bar."

Bradshaw spoke next and claimed the Court should sentence Charles without delay.

Once again Charles asked if he would be allowed to "...speak freely or not," and Bradshaw stated that the Court would hear him but only if he answered "...the matter that is charged upon you."

Charles launched into a long speech, which Bradshaw tried to interrupt. The King maintained that he sought to maintain the ancient laws of the Kingdom and maintain the liberties of his people. He referred to the talks he had had with Parliament and said, "How I came here, I know not. There is no law for it to make your King a prisoner."

Bradshaw was at last successful in interrupting the King and asked that Charles acknowledge the authority of the Court and give his answer.

The Clerk of the Court repeated the charge once more and said, "...the Court now requires you to give your positive and final answer, by way of confession or denial of the charge."

Charles responded by yet again denying the legality of the Court, which resulted in Bradshaw's ordering the King to be removed. During the final exchange of words, Bradshaw said that the King should understand that he was before a Court of Justice, to which the King replied, "I see I am before a power."

The Court had already come to its, as yet unannounced, decision that the King was guilty of the charges and because of this, it was not deemed necessary to call any witnesses to the Court. To reinforce their case, however, the Court was not reconvened on the Wednesday and Thursday and the Commissioners spent this time in the Painted Chamber, hearing in private the evidence of witnesses. This was little more than a gesture and consisted mostly of evidence from soldiers who were able to state that the King had taken part in the Wars. Enough evidence was gathered this way to convince the Commissioners that the King was guilty of the charges made against him, although most of them had probably already made up their minds on this before the trial even started.

On the Thursday, the Commissioners resolved that the Court would

"...proceed to sentence of Condemnation against Charles Stuart, King of England...That the condemnation of the King shall be for a tyrant, traitor and murderer...That the condemnation of the King shall be likewise for being a public enemy to the Commonwealth of England...That condemnation shall extend to death."

The Commissioners present also directed that all the members of the Court who,

"...are in and about London and are not present now be summoned to attend the service of this court the morrowe at one of the clock in the afternoon. For whom summonses were issued forth accordingly."

The Commissioners, once again, tried to anticipate the actions of the King and they determined that on the last day of the trial:

"That in case the king shall submit to the jurisdiction of this court and pray a copy of the charge that then the court do withdraw and advise...

That in case the king shall move anything else worth the court's consideration, that the lord president upon advice of the said assistants, do give orders for the courts withdrawing to advise...

That in case the King shall not submit to answer and there happens to be no such cause of withdrawing, that then the lord president do command the sentence to be read; but that the lord president should hear the King say what he would before the sentence and not after."

Bradshaw now had clear guidelines for his handling of the final proceedings of the court, and ones which he followed to the letter.

When the Court opened on Saturday 27th January, which was to be its last day, Charles did not wait for the proceedings to be formally opened, but began to speak at once.

"I shall desire a word to be heard a little, and I hope I shall give no occasion of interruption."

Bradshaw, who was determined that Charles should not be heard first, told the King that he would be allowed to speak later.

Charles reluctantly gave way on this point. Earlier that day, Bradshaw had received a rebuke from his wife, who in tears, begged him to have nothing to do with the sentencing of the King, "...for fear of the dreadful sentences of the King of Heaven."

Bradshaw replied, "I confess he hath done me no harm, nor will I do him any, but what the Law commands."

The proceedings for the day were then formally opened. Bradshaw told the Court that the prisoner had been asked several times to answer the charges of treason and other crimes in the name of the people of England. At this point a masked lady in the Gallery shouted, "Not half, not a quarter of the people of England! Oliver Cromwell is a traitor!" One of the officers ordered the soldiers present to level their muskets at the box from which the words were spoken, but when it was discovered that the culprit was Lady Fairfax, she was persuaded to leave the Court before she caused any further disorder.

When the Court had been silenced following this disturbance, Bradshaw continued and stated that as the King had not pleaded, he must be regarded as having confessed and that the Court could agree on the sentence. Bradshaw told the King he could still speak in his defence, as long as he did not continue to question the Court's power.

Charles repeated, yet again, his attitude to the Court and asked that he be heard by the Lords and Commons in the Painted Chamber before any sentence was passed. Charles was likely to accept the full Parliament of

Lords *and* Commons as a court of law. The King's request caused a disturbance amongst the Commissioners and Bradshaw was forced to suspend the sitting of the Court.

The Commissioners argued amongst themselves for half an hour outside the Court. Many were unhappy with the legality of the proceedings and agreed with the King in his questioning of the legal authority of the Court. Some of the Commissioners were, in later years, to assert that they had spoken out at this time for the King. There was clearly a major disagreement amongst the Commissioners and some of the more forceful members were in no mood for further debate at this stage of the trial. Their arguments, or whatever other tactics they may have used, meant that they had reached an agreement or at least a mutual understanding.

The main voice of protest was from John Downes who said,

> "God knows I desire not the king's death but his life. All that I thirst after is the settlement of the nation in peace. His Majesty doth now offer it and in order to it desires to speak with his Parliament."

Cromwell spoke against Downes, who left the Painted Chamber in tears. Despite his outburst, he had been weak enough to allow himself to be brow-beaten into sitting as a Commissioner and was also weak enough to add his signature to the King's Death Warrant. If any others thought the same as Downes, they kept silent and towed the party line.

When the Court was reassembled, Bradshaw accused the King of attempting to delay judgement and he refused to call a meeting of the Lords and Commons to hear the King. Bradshaw announced that the Court would proceed to the sentence.

Charles answered in a resigned manner, "Sir I know it is in vain for me to dispute, I am no sceptic for to deny the power that you have." He then proceeded to ask again for the opportunity to present a new plan for the peace of the Nation, which he allowed might cause some delay in the proceedings,

> "...but a little delay of a day or two further may give peace, wheras a hasty judgement may bring on that trouble and perpetual inconveniency to the Kingdom, that the child that is unborn may repent it."

It is thought that the King may have intended to propose his abdication from the throne in favour of his eldest son. Bradshaw, however, refused to hear the King's intentions and declared that the Court would now continue.

"Sir," said the King, "I have nothing more to say but I shall desire that this may be entered, what I have said."

Bradshaw had obviously taken much time to prepare his closing speech, which was to last for forty minutes. He began by detailing the principles for which the War had been fought and placed much emphasis on the legal and historical justification for the trial, giving many examples of how earlier Kings had been held answerable for their crimes.

He told the King,

> "you are the twenty-fourth King from William the Conqueror, you shall find more than one half of them have come in by the state and not merely on the point of descent."

Bradshaw quoted the scriptures and that Genesis 9, 35 stated that if,

> "...innocent blood that has been shed, whereby indeed the land still stands defiled with that blood, and as the text has it, it can no way be cleansed but with the shedding of the blood of him that shed this blood."

Bradshaw's crucial point was that

> "there is a contract and a bargain made between the King and his People, and your oath is taken, and certainly, Sir, the bond is reciprocal; for as you are the liege lord, so they liege subjects...This we know now, the one tie, the one bond, is the bond of protection that is due from the Sovereign; the other is the bond of subjection that is due from the subject. Sir, if this bond be once broken, farewell Sovereignty."

The Charge against the King was repeated. Bradshaw urged the King to implore God's forgiveness for blood guiltiness.

Charles interrupted angrily desiring,

> "...one word before you give sentence and that is that you would hear me concerning those great imputations that you have laid to my charge."

This request was refused. The King was told that as he had refused to acknowledge the Court, it need not hear one word from him.

The sentence against the King was read.

"Whereas the Commons of England in Parliament had appointed then a High Court of Justice, for the trying of Charles Stuart, King of England, before whom he had been three times convened; and at the first time a charge of High Treason, and other crimes and misdemeanours was read on the behalf of the Kingdom of England...

...An that by the said cruell and unnatural warres so levied, continued and renewed, much innocent blood of the free people of this nation hath bin split, many families undone, the publique treasure wastes and exhausted, trade obstructed and miserably decayed, vast expense and damage to the nation incurred and many parts of the land spoyled, some of them even unto desolation... And that hee thereby hath bin, and is, the occasioner, author and contriver of the said unnatural, cruell and blouddy warrs, and therein guilty of all the treasons, murthers, rapines, burnings, spoyles, desolations, damage and mischeefe to this nation, acted and committed in the said warrs or occasioned thereby...

Which charge being read unto him, as aforesaid, he the said Charles Stuart was required to give his answer; but he refused to do so; and so expresses the several passages of his trial in refusing to answer. For all which treasons and crimes this Court doth adjudge, that the said Charles Stuart, as a tyrant, traitor, murderer, and a public enemy, shall be put to death, by the severing his head from his body."

At the conclusion of the reading, all the Commissioners present rose to their feet to signify their agreement.

Legally a prisoner condemned to death was considered already dead and was not allowed to speak after the sentence. This was upheld by Bradshaw.

"Will you hear me a word, Sir?" asked the King.

"Sir, you are not to be heard after the sentence," was Bradshaw's response.

"No, Sir," replied the King, who appeared dismayed that his trial had ended so abruptly. He had fully expected to be able to speak again after the sentence, but saw, too late, that his last chance had gone. He found himself condemned as guilty simply by his silence.

Bradshaw ordered the prisoner to be removed and Charles was led away still demanding to be heard. "I am not suffered for to speak; expect what justice other people will have."

The King left the Court to cries from the soldiers present (on the orders of their officers) of "Execution! Justice! Execution!"

"Poor creatures," said Charles with a smile, "for a sixpence they would say as much of their own commanders."

As he passed by some of the soldiers, they scoffed at him and blew smoke from their pipes into his face; others spat upon him. Charles was taken, in a closed sedan chair, not back to Cotton House, but to Whitehall. There, the soldiers had been removed from his bedchamber at the request of Herbert, who in the last days of the King was to show, within the limits of his loyalty to the Army, much concern and sympathy for him.

Charles had ordered his two dogs, a spaniel and a greyhound, to be removed from his chambers, as he did not want them to disturb his composure. He did not know how long he would have before he would face his death, but he was certain that it would not be long. He now needed to turn to his God for comfort and strength.

Foreign ambassadors appealed on behalf of the King and a letter from the Queen was left unopened by the Commissioners. The Prince of Wales sent a blank piece of paper, which bore only his signature at the bottom, to consent to any terms necessary to save his father's life. All was in vain, the irreversible sentence had been passed and all that remained now was for it to be carried out.

V   PREPARATIONS

It was well past one o'clock in the afternoon of Tuesday 30th January, when Charles, anointed King of England, Ireland, Scotland and France, Defender of the Faith, stepped through a window of the Banqueting House in Whitehall onto the scaffold. The time had come.

Charles had risen early that morning, between five and six o'clock. He woke Thomas Herbert, who was sleeping on a pallet at his bedside.

"I will get up," said Charles, "I have a great work to do this day."

It had been only three days since Charles had received the sentence of the Court. The Commissioners had agreed on the 26th that the King was to be sentenced to death and the Warrant had already been drawn up. By the end of the day it had already received some twenty-eight signatures. More signatures were added on the 27th and finally, on Monday 29th, the Warrant was taken to the Painted Chamber where, possibly after Oliver Cromwell and others had uttered a number of threats, most of the remaining Commissioners added their seals and signatures to the document. Ultimately fifty-nine out of the sixty-seven Commissioners who had pronounced judgement on the King signed and sealed the Warrant. (See Appendix II for a full list of the signatories).

By 29th January, however, the Warrant was out of date. Obviously the Court had anticipated an earlier end to the trial. It was probably considered hazardous to attempt to draw up a second document which would have needed another signature from all the Commissioners, many of whom may well have already left London. Alterations were made to the date of the Warrant and the names of two new army officers were substituted for the two, now unknown, officers whose names had originally appeared. It can only be assumed that, at the last minute, the original officers had refused to have anything to do with the execution of the King.

The Warrant still survives and the alterations can be clearly seen. In the following quotes from the Warrant, the alterations and new insertions are shown in italics. Letters in square brackets represent contractions or abbreviations in the original.

In its final form, it was directed to three officers of the Army:

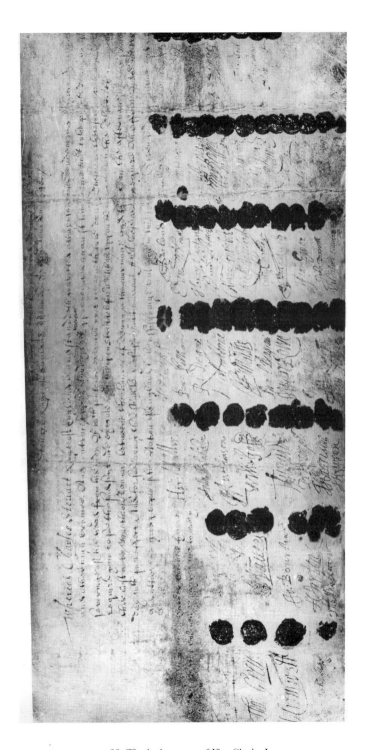

23. *The death warrant of King Charles I.*

"To Colonell Francis Hacker, Colonell Huncks and Lieutenant Colonell Phayre and to every one of them.

At the high Co[ur]t of Justice for the tryinge and judginge of Charles Steuart Kinge of England January xxixth Anno D[omi]ni 1648.
Whereas Charles Steuart Kinge of England is and standeth convicted attaynted and condemned of High Treason and other high Crymes, And sentence *uppon Saturday last was* pronounced against him by this Co[ur]t to be put to death by the severinge of his head from his body Of w[hi]ch sentence execuc[i]on yet remayneth to be done, These are therefore to will and require you to see the said sentence executed *In the* open Streete before Whitehall upon the morrowe, being the Thirtieth day of this instante moneth of January, betweene the houres of Tenn in the morninge and *Five* in the afternoone of the same day w[i]th full effect And for soe doing this shall be yo[u]r sufficient warrant And these are to require all Officers and Souldiers and other good people of this Nation of England to be assistinge unto *you* in this service..."

Note: At this time, a new year was held to start on the 25th March, not on the first of January. This means that the date on the warrant of 29th January is correctly shown as 1648 and not 1649 as it would be reckoned today.

The Warrant remained in the possession of Colonell Hacker. In 1660, after the restoration of Charles II, Hacker, then a prisoner in the Tower of London, was ordered by the House of Lords to surrender the Warrant to them. This was done and the Warrant has remained in the custody of the House of Lords ever since. Until 1851 it was preserved in the Jewel Tower at Westminster and since then it has been in the House of Lords Library. It has faded somewhat over the centuries, but under ultra-violet light it is still fully legible, although it is not possible to make out the words which have been erased. On the back of the Warrant is written in a seventeenth century hand: "The bloody Warr[an]t for murthering the King."

On 29th January the Commissioners issued a further directive:

"...that the officers of the ordinance within the Towre of London, or any other officer or officer of the store within the Towre of London, or any other officers within the said Towre in whose hands or custody the bright execution ax for the executing malifactors is, doe forthwith deliver unto Edward Dendy Esquir. Serient at Armes attending this court, or his deputie or deputies, the said axe, and for theire or either of theire soe doing, this shall be theire warrant."

It is apparent from this that there was one special axe kept at the Tower of London which was used solely for judicial decapitations. In all probability, it was this axe which had been used to execute such notables as the Earl of Strafford in 1641 and Archbishop Laud in 1645.

It is not possible to identify with any certainty the axe today as the Tower does not have any pre-Civil War inventories which distinguish an execution axe. The first inventory which makes this distinction is dated 1676. The heading axe now on display at the Tower has been identified using this inventory. Axes are particularly difficult to date, but this axe is usually identified as being of the sixteenth century and it may, therefore, be the very same "bright ax".

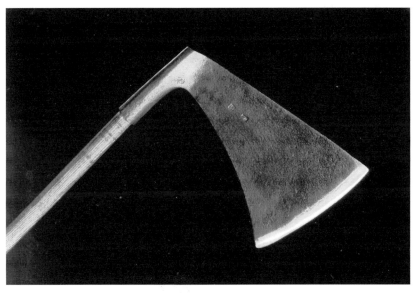

24. The execution axe in the Tower of London.

The Earl of Holland and Lord Capel were executed not long after Charles and, on enquiry of the Headsman, Lord Capel was assured that the same axe was to be used as had been used to execute the King. This confirms the idea that there was only the one special execution axe held in the Tower Armouries.

Tower Hill was the usual site chosen for public executions and many well-known public figures met their end there. Special stands were often erected to accommodate the vast crowds which turned out for such a special event.

For the execution of the King, Tower Hill would have probably been the expected choice, but the site finally chosen was at Whitehall, in the area outside the Banqueting House. This area was much smaller than the space available at Tower Hill, but for this reason was considered to be more secure as it could be easily guarded. Parliament did not want a last-minute rescue attempt and security was of the utmost importance.

Later on the 29th, one of the many news sheets of the time, *The Moderate*, reported that, "Scaffolds are this day building and will be all night, in order to the King's execution." The same report stated that the Commissioners had, "...voted that the place of execution should be over against the Banqueting House of Whitehall."

The news spread fast. *The Kingdom's Weekly Intelligencer* of the same date reported of the King that,

"...his children are now with him, howsoever it is believed on to-morrow he will suffer, and to that purpose, the way is now railed in from Whitehall to the Great Gate as you go to King's Street, about the middle wherof it is said the scaffold will be erected."

A contemporary engraving by Hollar helps to explain the meaning of these passages. It shows both the Banqueting House and the gate into Whitehall built in the reign of Henry VIII and known as the Holbein Gate. The view is drawn from the north. A line of posts, or bollards, runs from the north corner of the Banqueting House and turns at a right-angle to join the Holbein Gate. It is reasonable to suppose that the "rails" erected followed the line of these posts and that within that area, against the façade of the Banqueting House, the scaffold was erected.

The whole area outside the Banqueting House formed a square enclosed on three sides: on the east side, the Banqueting House itself, with the Holbein Gate entrance to the palace of Westminster to the south, and the blank wall of the old Tilt Yard to the east. The space was about one hundred and twenty feet wide. All the buildings around the space were part of the headquarters of the Army and were, therefore, secure. A battery of guns had already been placed on a platform built in the corner between the Banqueting House and the Holbein Gate. A fine modern model in the Museum of London, based on the Hollar drawing and contemporary plans, shows the Banqueting House and the surrounding buildings.

There has been much dispute as to which window of the Banqueting House gave access to the scaffold. The window the King used was above the original entrance to the Banqueting House, which was demolished in 1744. A new entrance was subsequently built on the same site and is the

25. Contemporary drawing by Hollar of the Banqueting House and the Holbein Gate at Whitehall.

one we see today. (See Appendix I for more information about this window and the Banqueting House).

The window was small and needed to be enlarged. There would have been a number of carpenters already on site, engaged in erecting the scaffold. It may have been necessary to remove the window frame and build steps leading down to a short walkway which was connected to the scaffold in front of the main façade of the Banqueting House.

Hammond, the Master carpenter at Whitehall was ordered to provide the scaffold. He employed one Robert Lockier to undertake this work and he was paid at the rate of 2s.6d. a day for his work. He would have needed a large number of workmen to fetch and carry and to saw and nail the large timbers used to make the scaffold.

At about five o'clock on the 29th the King was carried back to St. James's Palace where he would spend his last night. It is thought that he was moved from the Palace of Westminster so that he would not be disturbed by the constant hammering of the workmen there. The building of the scaffold would have continued throughout the night.

As Charles had anticipated, many people came to see him, including his nephew the Prince Elector, the Duke of Richmond, the Marquis of Hertford and the Earls Southampton and Lindsay, but Charles refused to see them.

William Juxon, Bishop of London was allowed to attend the King and was effectively placed under close guard with him. When the Bishop entered the King's room he started to condole with Charles.

The King stopped the Bishop, "Leave off this my Lord," he said to Juxon.

"We have not the time for it. Let us think of our great work and prepare to meet that great God, to whom ere long I am to give an account of myself. And I hope I shall do it with peace and that you

26. Modern model of the Banqueting House as it was in 1649, showing surrounding buildings and the location of the scaffold.

will assist me therein. We will not talk of these rogues in whose hands I am. They thirst after my blood and they will have it and God's will be done. I thank God I heartily forgive them and I will talk of them no more."

Charles was allowed to receive a messenger, Henry Seymour, from the Prince of Wales who was in Holland. The letter from the Prince was brief.

"I do not only pray for Your Majesty according to my duty, but shall always be ready to do all which shall be in my power to deserve that blessing which I now humbly beg of Your Majesty."

The King gave Bishop Juxon a letter for the Prince of Wales, in which he explained the

"...true glory of princes consists in advancing God's glory, in the maintenance of true religion and the Church's good; also in the dispensation of civil powere, with justice and honour to the public peace."

The King put his worldly affairs in order with Juxon, arranging with him a few legacies. Charles also burnt all his private letters which were with him, "which done his Majesty and Dr. Juxon did much rejoice."

The King amused himself by constructing an anagram from his title of "Carolus Rex." It was a prophetic phrase *"Cras ero lux"*, which means "tomorrow I will be the light" and indicates his thoughts at this time.

At St. James's Palace, Charles was allowed a final, if brief, meeting with two of his youngest children, Princess Elizabeth, aged thirteen and Prince Henry, Duke of Gloucester, aged eight, who were living at Sion House under the protection of Parliament. The Prince of Wales and his younger brother, James, Duke of York were in Holland, along with Charles's eldest daughter Mary, who was married to the Prince of Orange. Queen Henrietta Maria was in France with their youngest daughter, Princess Henrietta, who had been born in Exeter during the Civil War.

Charles told his children that he was glad they had come as he had feared he would not be allowed to see them or write to them. He stated that they should not grieve for him for he was to face a glorious death "...for the laws and liberties of this land and for maintaining the Protestant Religion." He recommended as reading to Princess Elizabeth several books, including Hooker's *Ecclesiastical Polity*, to give her a grounding against the evils of Popery.

The King said that he forgave all his enemies and asked his children to do the same, but not to trust them. Charles had no doubt that the throne would settle upon his eldest son and he impressed on Elizabeth and Henry that they should no longer look upon the Prince of Wales as their eldest brother, but as their Sovereign.

It must have been a distressing meeting for all, but Charles spoke plainly to his children and was anxious that they should know exactly what would happen to him the next day. "They will cut off my head," Charles said to Prince Henry and then told him that he must not allow Parliament to make him a King,

> "...so long as your brothers Charles and James do live for they will cut off your brother's heads and cut off thy head too at last. And therefore I charge you, do not be made a King by them."

"I will be torn in pieces first," was the young Prince's reply, which pleased Charles greatly.

Charles then gave his children the few personal belongings remaining with him, all that is apart from the George he wore (the insignia of the Order of the Garter) which he intended to wear to the scaffold.

Charles asked Elizabeth to tell her mother, Queen Henrietta Maria, "...that his love should be the same to the last."

He then kissed the Prince and Princess, gave them his blessing and bade them farewell. Charles turned away from them as they left the room with Bishop Juxon. He walked quickly into his bedchamber and lay down on the bed. Bishop Juxon observed that the King was visibly moved by the meeting and that his legs were trembling.

What was left of the evening was spent in prayer and quiet meditation with Bishop Juxon. Some time after darkness fell, the Bishop left, Charles having requested him to return early the next morning. Charles remained awake for a while, reading and praying until nearly midnight and then retired to bed. As usual his bedchamber was lit by a burning wax candle placed in a silver basin.

By the King's orders, Herbert brought his bed into the King's chamber. Herbert later stated that,

> "...for some hours his Majesty slept very soundly, for my part I was so full of anguish and grief that I took little rest. The King, some hours before day, drew back his bed curtains to awaken me and could by the light of the wax lamp perceive me troubled in my sleep."

VI   EXECUTION

The next morning Charles appeared to be calm, composed and prepared to face death.

"Herbert," he said, "this is my second marriage day; I would be as trim today as may be, for before night I hope to be espoused to my blessed Jesus."

Herbert helped Charles to dress and combed his long hair.

The January weather was severe, it being so cold that the river Thames had frozen over. The King put on an extra shirt as he was concerned that the cold might make him shiver and that anyone watching would think that he was afraid.

"Let me have a shirt more than ordinary, by reason the season is so sharp as probably make me shake, which some will imagine proceeds from fear. I would have no such imputation...I fear not death, said the King. Death is not terrible to me; I bless my God I am prepared."

Two shirts, reputedly the ones worn by the King on the day of his execution, still survive. One, probably the outer shirt worn by the King, is in the possession of her Majesty the Queen and is kept at Windsor Castle. The second, which is of blue knitted silk and which would have given the King the protection from the cold he desired, is in the Museum of London.

Bishop Juxon had arrived early that morning as Charles had requested and he was allowed to be alone with the King for about an hour. Then Herbert was called into the room and the Bishop said morning prayers and administered the Sacrament to the King. The Bishop read the lesson for the day, which was on the Passion of Christ. Charles thought that the Bishop had chosen this passage specially, but was told that it was the lesson ordained in the Prayer Book for that day. Charles was impressed and pleased by this news. Shortly after this, at about ten o'clock, Colonel Hacker knocked at the door, entered and told the King, "...in trembling fashion," that the time had come for him to leave for Whitehall.

27. The blue knitted silk shirt of Charles I, worn at his execution.

Charles put on his cloak, bearing the large silver star of the Order of the Garter, in readiness for the short walk from St. James's Palace to Whitehall.

The King at this time appears not to have known exactly where his execution was to take place, for he remarked that,

> "...he was glad it was to be done there rather than where he was, in regard it was a very cold morning and without a little motion he should be indisposed to what he intended to say."

Colonel Tomlinson met the King at St. James's Palace and walked, with his hat in his hand, on one side of him with Bishop Juxon on the other

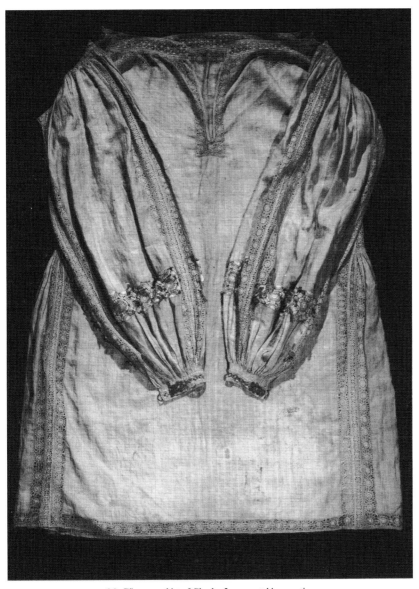

28. The outer shirt of Charles I, worn at his execution.

and with Herbert following. This small group was then immediately surrounded by two companies of infantry which had been drawn up in readiness at the Palace to provide an escort and guard.

The procession set off across the park, with drums beating loudly and colours flying. It was a dull, cold morning and the ground was hard with frost. Charles is reputed to have been a fast walker and is said to have asked the troops to set a faster pace.

With the constant noise of the drums, conversation would have been difficult on the journey, but Charles exchanged some words with Colonel Tomlinson and expressed the hope that the Duke of Richmond would be allowed to take care of his burial.

The party ascended a wooden staircase which led from the Park into the buildings of Whitehall. Walking along the gallery above the Tilt Yard, the King would have passed many family portraits and many of the paintings from his great art collection, collected in happier times. Charles crossed over the main street by the upper floor of the Holbein Gate, from which he may well have been able to see the scaffold and the waiting crowd.

The news-sheets of the day reported that the King arrived at Whitehall soon after ten o'clock.

Earlier that morning, the Commissioners of Parliament had met again and had issued another directive, that "...the scaffold upon which the Kinge is to be executed bee covered with blacke," which was duly done.

The day wore on. Charles had probably expected to be led to the scaffold early in the day, but he was to be kept cruelly waiting. The wait must have been extremely trying for the King, but all those around him remarked on his calmness. Midday arrived and a meal was prepared for him, but the offer of food was refused as the King had resolved to touch no food or drink after receiving the Sacrament. Bishop Juxon remonstrated with the Charles and finally persuaded him that he should eat at least something. If he ate nothing, Juxon argued, he might faint on the scaffold from the effects of the cold weather, and this might be interpreted by those watching as being caused by fear. This was the argument which convinced Charles, and he eventually ate about half a small loaf of white bread and drank a glass of claret. One account states that he initially asked for beer as he had not expected there to be any of his wines left in the cellars of Whitehall.

Contemporary accounts remarked on the King's courage, whilst waiting at the Banqueting House.

"The King himself showed a calm and composed firmness, which amazed all people, and that so much the more because it was not natural to him. It was imputed to a very extraordinary measure of supernatural assistance. Bishop Juxon did the duty of his function earnestly, but with a dry coldness that could not raise the King's thoughts; so that it was owing wholly to somewhat within himself that he went through so many indignities with so much true greatness, without disorder or any sort of affectation."

Charles spent much of his time praying with the Bishop. Other ministers arrived and desired to pray with the King. His reply, through Bishop Juxon, to their request was a refusal.

"Tell them plainly that they, that have so often and causelessly prayed against me, shall never pray with me in this agony. They may, if they please, and I'll thank them for it, pray for me."

The Commissioners were, at this time, facing another unforseen problem, as it had not been possible to find anyone to behead the King. Brandon, the official executioner, had been expected to perform the task, but when faced with the prospect of executing his Monarch, he had refused in horror, stating that he would be "...shot or otherwise killed, rather than do it." One must wonder if that is not *exactly* the threat that the Commissioners actually made to Brandon, when he refused to undertake his duty.

There has been much debate about the identity of the two headsmen who were eventually to appear on the scaffold with the King, and in particular on the identity of the man who actually wielded the axe. A written warrant would probably have been prepared at the time, issued by Hacker, Huncks or Phayre, the officers named on the Death Warrant as being responsible for arranging the execution. No documentary evidence has survived, and in its absence, the debate will continue. It is likely that any evidence was lost at the time of the Restoration of the Monarchy in 1660, when many of those involved in the events leading up to the execution of the King did their best to distance and disassociate themselves from it.

Eventually, in the late morning of the day of the execution, two men were found to perform the task. Both stipulated that they must be given a disguise, so that their identities should not be known. By the time the necessary disguises had been prepared and the headsmen made ready, it was between one and two o'clock in the afternoon, when the King was finally called to the scaffold.

It is sometimes stated that this delay was also caused by Parliament holding a last-minute sitting to pass an Act prohibiting the proclamation of the Prince of Wales as King. On the previous Saturday, however,

Parliament had passed an act prohibiting anyone from being proclaimed King. On the actual day of the execution, many members of the House deemed it prudent to be absent from the City.

When at last the King appeared on the scaffold, the sun had broken through the clouds and was shining brightly. The brightness must have seemed all the more intense to Charles, who emerged from the relative gloom of the Banqueting House, where many windows had been blocked during the Wars. Charles may have walked beneath the splendid painted ceiling he commissioned from Rubens, with its scenes glorifying his father James I.

The area outside the Banqueting House was packed. The space between the scaffold and the rails was filled with soldiers; outside the rails troops of horses mixed with the waiting crowd and filled the streets. Every possible precaution had been taken to prevent any rescue attempt and also to ensure that any speech or appeal made by the King would go unheard by the public, who were placed beyond the ranks of soldiers and would have been able to see little and hear even less. Many people managed to climb onto the rooftops of the surrounding buildings and tried to approach as close as they were allowed.

In the centre of the scaffold, opposite the middle window of the Banqueting House, stood the block: a billet of wood about eighteen inches long and six inches in height, flat at the bottom and rounded at the top. Near the block, on the floor of the scaffold, lay the axe.

Four heavy iron staples had been driven into the wooden floor of the scaffold, which was littered with rope. The rope and staples were there to be used if the King decided to resist and needed to be forcibly dragged down onto the block. This also accounted for the unusual lowness of the block. A cheap deal coffin, which cost "but six shillings" lay to one side and a black velvet pall to cover the coffin lay in readiness. The floor of the scaffold had been sprinkled with sand, to soak up any blood and to prevent anyone from slipping after the execution had taken place.

The small platform was crowded with people. Colonel Tomlinson and Bishop Juxon had come onto the scaffold with the King. At the King's request, Herbert remained within the Banqueting House. Herbert was upset at being left behind, but he had been visibly distressed for much of the morning and Charles was probably concerned that Herbert's presence might disturb his own composure on the scaffold. Colonel Hacker was there formally to see the sentence of the Court carried out, along with several soldiers on guard. Also there were two or three shorthand writers with notebooks and ink horns, to record the King's last words.

The two headsmen awaited the King, both wearing their disguises. One (who was later to hold aloft the King's severed head) wore a large hat

29. Charles I on the scaffold: 19th century painting by Ernest Crofts.

"cocked up" and the second (who wielded the axe) had on a "grey grisled periwig which hung down very low" and a "grey beard". In addition, both wore masks covering the whole face and they were dressed in close woollen "frocks", garments worn at the time by butchers and sailors.

The author of *The Perfect Weekly Account* wrote of Charles that, "...no man could have come with more confidence and appearance of resolution" upon the scaffold than did the King,

> "...viewing the block, with the axe lying upon it, and iron staples in the scaffold to bind him down upon the block in case he had refused to submit himself freely, without being anyway daunted. Yea, when the deputies of that grim Serjeant Death appeared with a terrifying disguise, the King with a pleasant countenance said he freely forgave them."

Charles had been denied the right to speak freely at his trial after the sentence had been passed, but he was allowed to speak, at some length, on the scaffold.

John Dillingham wrote in his publication the *Moderate Intelligencer*,

> "...at his first coming he lookt upon the people who were numerous, as also the souldiers. Little appeared in the faces of any, either of joy or sorrow, those who had most cause to mourn, as greatest losers, being absent."

The King removed a small piece of paper from his pocket, on which he had written some brief notes. His last words were spoken to the fifteen or so people present on the scaffold.

> "I shall be very little heard of anyone here...I shall therefore speak a word unto you here. Indeed I could hold my peace very well, but I think it is my duty to God first and to my country, for to clear myself both as an honest man, a good King and a good Christian."

Charles insisted that he had not begun the Civil War and that he considered his sentence illegal. He added that he regarded his sentence as just punishment by God for, "...an unjust sentence that I suffered to take effect, is punished now by an unjust sentence on me." Although Charles did not mention any name, he was making reference to his allowing the execution of Strafford, earlier in his reign.

During the course of his speech, Charles became concerned that the axe might be damaged, with all the obstacles on the floor and the number of people there, "...one standing so neer the axe that his cloke touch'd it," which resulted in the King saying, "Do not hurt the axe, though it may me." Charles continued and went on to forgive his enemies and he spoke of his people.

"Truly I desire their liberty and freedom as much as anybody whomsoever, but I must tell you their liberty and freedom consists in having of government, those laws by which their life and their goods may be most their own. It is not for having a share in government, Sir, that is nothing pertaining to them. A subject and Sovereign are clear different things...it was for this that now I am come here. If I would have given way to an arbitrary way, for to have all laws changed according to the power of the sword, I needed not to have come here; and therefore I tell you (and I pray God it be not laid to your charge) that I am a martyr of the people."

Charles would have ended his speech here, but Bishop Juxon reminded him that he should say something about his religion, so the King, suitably prompted, added,

"...I die a Christian according to the profession of the Church of England as I found it left me by my father...I have a good cause and I have a gracious God: I will say no more."

His speech ended, the King prepared for death. He spoke to the two headsmen. There is no account of the exact words, but he explained to them that he would kneel with his head on the block and would pray briefly and then make a sign for the blow to be struck. He asked how he should arrange his long hair so as not to impede the axe. With the help of Bishop Juxon he put on a cap and pushed his hair up beneath it.

"There is but one stage more," said Juxon,

"which though turbulent and troublesome, yet it is a very short one; you may consider that it will carry you a very great way; it will carry you from Earth to Heaven, and there you shall find to your great joy, the prize you hasten to; a Crown of Glory."

Charles replied, "I go from a corruptible to an incorruptible Crown, where no disturbance can be, no disturbance in the world."

Charles then gave away the last of his few remaining possessions. He gave his George to Bishop Juxon, with the word "Remember". It is thought that the Bishop had been instructed to give the insignia of the Order of the Garter to the Prince of Wales, although it was never to reach him. The

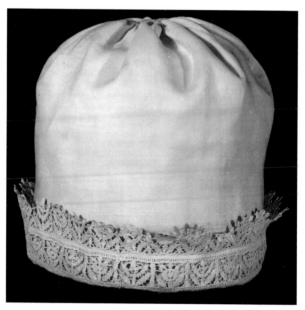

30. Cap of Charles I, similar to the one he wore on the scaffold.

31. The doublet reputed to have been worn by Charles I on the scaffold

32. Fragment of the cloak said to have been worn by Charles I on the scaffold, with contemporary authentication.

jewel was confiscated from Juxon after the execution and was later sold at auction.

Charles gave his cane to the Bishop. His silver watch and his gold watch were left to the Duke of Richmond (the gold watch being meant for the Duchess). His striking clock he bequeathed to Herbert.

Charles then removed his doublet, and temporarily replaced his cloak against the cold. He looked at the block and asked if it was set fast and regretted that it was so low. The executioner, probably being unwilling to explain why it was so low, simply said, "It can be no higher, Sir."

Charles stood for a moment, praying in silence. He then slipped off his cloak and lay down with his head on the block. One of the headsmen bent down to ensure that the King's hair was not in the way, and thinking the blow was about to be struck, Charles said "Stay for the sign!"

"I will an'it please Your Majesty," was the reply.

After a few seconds, the King stretched out his hands. The "bright ax" flashed and at one blow, Charles's head was severed from his body.

Few people would have seen the blow strike, as when the King lay down on the block he would have been visible only to those who surrounded him on the scaffold and to those on the surrounding buildings. The rails of the scaffold were probably draped with black material which would have prevented the public's view.

The second headsman held up Charles's severed head to the crowd, which gave, in the words of one eyewitness, "...such a groan as I have never heard before, and I desire I may never hear again."

It was customary practice at public executions for the severed head to be held up to the crowd, with the cry of "behold the head of a traitor". Many writers have asserted that this cry was given, but one account by an eyewitness specifically states that the executioner said nothing, and none of the other publications of the time disagree with this. That the cry was not given can be taken as evidence that the executioner was not familiar with the task, or, as was more likely, that he was afraid to call out for fear that his voice might be recognised.

According to Sir William Sanderson, who witnessed the execution of the King, the fatal blow was struck within one minute of two o'clock.

Projicis inventum caput Angla Ecclesia ? Cæsum
Si caput est, salvum corpus an esse potest?

Peter Huybrechts *fecit et Exc.*

33.Contemporary illustration of the execution of Charles I.

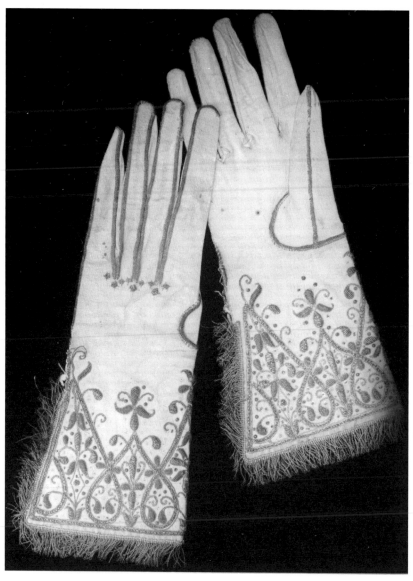

34. Gloves, reputedly worn by the King on the scaffold and given to Bishop Juxon.

VII   THE KING IS DEAD

After the blow from the axe severed the King's head, two troops of horse advanced towards the Banqueting House, one from the north, the second from the south, scattering the crowds before them. Within half an hour of the execution the area outside the Banqueting House was empty.

One witness, Sir William Dugdale, wrote afterwards on what happened after the axe had fallen. He noted in his diary for that day,

"His head was thrown down by him that took it up. Bruised the face. His hair was cut off. Soldiers dipped their swords in his blood. Base language upon his dead body."

Mercurius Elenctius, a Royalist publication issued on 7th February said,

"When they had murdered him, such as desired to dip their handkerchiefs or other things in his blood, were admitted for monies. Others brought pieces of board which were dy'd with his blood, for which the soldiers took of some a shilling, of others half a crowne, according to the quality of the person that sought it. But none without ready money. And after his body was coffin'd as many as desired to see it were permitted at a certain rate, by which the soldiers got store of moneys, insomuch that one was heard to say 'I wish we had two or three more Majesties to behead, if we could but make such use of them.'"

Sir Roger Manley wrote,

"They were inhumanly barbarous to his dead corpse. His hair and blood were sold by parcels. Their hands and sticks were tinged with his blood and the block, now cut into chips, as also the sand, sprinkled with his sacred gore, were exposed for sale, which were greedily bought, but for different ends, by some as trophies of their slain enemy, and by others as precious relics of their beloved Prince."

*35. A reliquary containing a lock of hair of
Charles I.*

These accounts may well have been elaborated as Royalist propaganda, but nevertheless do ring true. Throughout history people have always taken full advantage of any opportunity to make some money and here was one not to be missed.

Charles's decapitated body and his head were placed in the coffin which had lain ready on the scaffold. The black velvet pall, which had also lain in readiness, was used to cover the coffin which was carried back into the Banqueting House under the guidance of Bishop Juxon and Thomas Herbert.

The King's body lay at Whitehall that night. Sir Purback Temple went there to view the body, as did many others, and gave "half a piece" to be allowed to do so. He wrote later,

> "Axtell, that then kept it, in a scoffing manner took me by the hand and said, 'If thou thinkest there is any sanctity or holiness in it look here,' where I saw the head of the blessed martyr'd King, lie in a coffin with his body, which smiled as perfectly as if it had been alive."

Clarendon stated that the body, "...was exposed for many days to the public view, that all men might know that he was not alive."

The headsmen left Whitehall immediately after the execution. After the Restoration of Charles II in 1660 there were many enquiries made as to the identity of the headsmen and statements were taken from those present at the execution. One Abraham Smith, a Thames waterman stated:

"...My Lord, as soon as the fatal blow was given, I was walking about Whitehall. Down came a file of musketeers. The first word they said was 'Where be the bargemen?', answer was made 'Here are none'. Away they directed the hangman into my boat. He gave one of the soldiers a crown. Saith the soldiers, 'Waterman, away with him, begone quickly'".

The unknown passenger denied that he had executed the King, but the Waterman said that, "...he shook, every joint of him."

It may be worth commenting here that whoever was the headsman who wielded the axe, he had done a very professional job. To sever a head with an axe in one clean blow required great skill and there were many instances where experienced headsmen took several blows to complete their task. It was also common for their victims to offer some additional payment if the executioner completed his task swiftly. It must be questioned if anyone unused to such a task could have performed so well on their first attempt, and especially at such an important occasion. Perhaps the headsman was the official executioner Brandon after all, who had been persuaded to perform the task for which he was the most qualified. Parliament may well have made him an offer he could not refuse.

Charles's body still lay at Whitehall on the 31st January. On 1st February the body was embalmed by a Maidstone surgeon, Thomas Trapham. Trapham was later made Surgeon to Oliver Cromwell and was probably the surgeon who embalmed *his* body in 1658.

The embalming of the King was reputedly performed on the large table in the Dean of Westminster's kitchen, although no records or documents survive to enable this story to be confirmed.

After removing the internal organs and cleaning the body, which must have still been covered in dried blood, the head of the King was sewn back onto the body. Trapham was later to make the remark that he had, "Sewed on the head of a goose".

Trapham was beset with requests for locks of hair and other relics. He was to say later that he refused to comply with them, although this must be considered doubtful. Many people still requested to see the King's body, either out of reverence or curiosity, but few were admitted at this time.

Trapham had removed all the clothes from the King's body. We know that this was done, for the two shirts reputedly worn by the King still survive. A doublet, reputedly that worn by the King on the scaffold also survives, at Longleat House, home of the Thynne family. It is made of pale blue silk. It came into the Thynne family in the eighteenth century from the granddaughter of the Earl of Hertford who was one of the Lords who had assisted with the burial of the King.

After the embalming, the body was wrapped in cere cloth and placed in a wooden coffin, the same coffin, no doubt, as was used to convey the body from the scaffold. It would have been unnecessary to make a new and more substantial coffin.

It is doubtful if the cheap deal coffin would have been pitched, padded and lined with silk. It would have become heavily blood-stained when the body was first placed in it immediately after execution. It may have been cleaned and lined ready to receive the embalmed body, but this is unlikely.

It was probably at this time that the wood coffin was closed and sealed in a lead shell as it had been two days since the execution. Herbert's account clearly states that the lead coffin was sealed after the embalming, although it is possible that the wooden coffin may have been left open for a further short period before finally being closed. No elaborate outer coffin was provided for the King and the lead coffin remained uninscribed.

It is sometimes related that Oliver Cromwell viewed the body of the King and this has been the subject of great discussion. As C.V. Wedgwood states in her account of the trial and execution in her book *The Trial of Charles I*, "...when history fails to supply the moment of drama, human invention will often fill the gap."

A so-called death-mask of Charles I is today on display in the Armoury at Hatfield House, home of Lord Salisbury. It appears to have been made out of metal and is bronze in colour. The features appear to be those of the King. The age of the mask is not known and it seems to have been omitted in all the inventories of the contents of the house. It is certain it has been at the House since 1840 which is when the Armoury was rearranged. The mask is placed inside a helmet of a period suit of armour.

This mask is almost certainly *not* a death-mask of the King. If such an important object was made and had survived, it would certainly have been known in Restoration England. Death-masks were usually made of plaster. No such mask seems to have been made from Charles's head, nor do any accounts of the time mention one. Interestingly enough, a death mask *was* made of Oliver Cromwell which still survives.

On the day the embalming was completed, the coffined body was moved from Whitehall to St. James's Palace.

Some days passed before Parliament gave the order to allow the King's burial. It would seem that no definite plans for the burial had been made before the execution, which was a curious oversight.

The nearest and most obvious place for the burial to be made was in Westminster Abbey. Both parents of the King, James I and Queen Anne of Denmark, were buried there, although in separate vaults. James I was interred in the small vault containing the bodies of King Henry VII and his Queen, beneath Henry VII's Chapel. The founder of the Stuart Dynasty was laid to rest with the founder of the earlier Tudor Dynasty.

Opening the vault in Westminster Abbey would have been relatively easy. It was usual for the internal organs (removed during the embalming process) to be buried almost immediately after the embalming had been completed. We know that a separate canopic chest was not buried with the King's body, so could it have been buried in Westminster whilst the deliberations on the place of burial were still being made? Sadly, the archives of the Abbey are completely missing for the period 1643 to 1659, so the records of the opening of any vaults are missing.

Objections to the use of Westminster Abbey as the place of burial were raised in the House of Commons. Parliament was not happy with the idea of the King's being buried in such a famous and accessible place. They did not want to see any tomb becoming a place of pilgrimage or a site for demonstrations on their own doorstep. Parliament declared that,

"...his burying there would attract infinite numbers of all sorts thither, to see where the King was buried; which was judged unsafe and inconvenient."

Parliament eventually decided that St. George's Chapel at Windsor would be a suitable burial site and preparations were put in hand. The Chapel, within the Castle at Windsor, was secure and unnecessary visitors could be excluded. The location was considered sufficiently remote from London. It was also the site where Henry VIII and many earlier monarchs had been buried, so there was a precedent for its use as a royal burial place.

The request for this site to be considered may well have been made by Bishop Juxon and Herbert. Charles himself had expressed no wish to be buried in any particular place and neither Bishop Juxon nor Herbert had thought fit to raise the matter with him in the days before the execution.

The formal order for the burial was given to Herbert and Anthony Mildmay, "...in any place within Windsor Castle, that they should think fit and meet."

Meanwhile the news of the execution spread quickly and was reported in all the news-sheets of the time. Sadly, the news took the longest time to reach those who were most deeply concerned. Rumours were rife, but the Prince of Wales, in The Hague, did not hear the facts until 4th February.

The news was broken to the Prince by one of his Chaplains, who simply addressed Charles as "Your Majesty". Charles immediately understood the meaning of these words and retired to his bedchamber in

36. St. George's Chapel at Windsor Castle.

a passionate outburst of grief. Since he had been little more than a child he had fought on land and sea in support of his father's cause, but now all seemed lost and his own position and future uncertain.

Queen Henrietta Maria, who was in France, did not hear of her widowhood until 9th February.

VIII   BURIAL

As Charles had wished, the Duke of Richmond was put in charge of the funeral arrangements, the cost of which, Parliament dictated, should not amount to more than five hundred pounds.

This sum was adequate, but certainly not excessive, by the standards of the time. The King's body had to be moved to Windsor and suits of mourning ordered for about twenty people.

The funeral was to be a quiet small affair and certainly not the full occasion of State which would have been expected had the King died under normal circumstances. Charles was to be given a decent burial, but one more suited to an ordinary member of the lesser nobility, than to a monarch.

Parliament declared that the body of the King, "...should be privately carried to Windsor without pomp or noise."

On 7th February, Herbert and Anthony Mildmay, with the assistance of John Joiner, conveyed the body of the King to Windsor. The journey took place at night and few people would have seen the procession either leave St. James's Palace or arrive at Windsor Castle. The King's coach containing the coffin was hung with black material, as were the four coaches which followed containing the King's servants. Two troops of Horse accompanied the coaches.

Upon arrival at Windsor Castle, the coffin was carried from the coach into the hall of the Dean's house. The hall was draped with black material and the coffin lay briefly there before it was carried into the King's bedchamber.

Herbert and Mildmay visited St. George's Chapel to determine the best place for the burial of the King. Their initial choice was the Wolsey Chapel, but this was rejected for two reasons. Firstly, it was not part of the main Chapel, where other Kings were buried, and secondly, because they thought that Henry VIII was buried there, and therefore considered it unsuitable for Charles to lie in the same vault as the King who had dissolved the monasteries and, in their opinion squandered,

"...those vast revenues, the suppressed abbies, monasteries, and other religious houses were endowed with, and by demolishing those many beautiful and stately structures, which both expressed the greatness of their founders, and preserved the splendour of the kingdom, which might at the Reformation in some measure have been kept up and converted to sundry pious uses."

Herbert and Mildmay failed to agree on a burial site but Richmond arrived at Windsor on 8th February. He was accompanied by three other noblemen who had attended the King throughout the last years of the war and for much of his period of imprisonment. They were Hertford, Lindsay and Southampton, so Herbert and Mildmay deferred to the opinion of the Lords on the burial place.

The four Lords then visited St. George's Chapel to decide on the exact location for the interment and to make the necessary arrangements. When they entered the Chapel they found that the Governor of the Castle, Colonel Whichcot, had already arranged for a grave to be excavated in the floor of the Chapel, near the tomb of Edward IV on the north side of the high altar. The location of this grave was instantly rejected by the Peers who wished to lay the body of King Charles in a more prominent position in the Chapel. They had hoped it could be laid in one of the vaults where the bones of earlier Kings were known to rest.

It had, however, been over one hundred years since any royal burials had been made in the Chapel and there were some doubts as to the precise location of the burial vaults. Walking up the choir, they managed to locate one vault by stamping their feet and tapping the floor with their sticks until they heard a hollow sound.

Then they

"...caused the place to be opened, it being near to the seats and opposite the eleventh stall on the Sovereign's side, in which were two coffins, one very large of King Henry VIII, the other of Queen Jane, his third wife, bothe covered with velvet palls, which seemed fresh though they had lain there above one hundred years."

It appeared that the vault was intended to hold one more body, probably that of Queen Katherine. Katherine Parr was Henry's sixth wife, but after his death she remarried and is buried at Sudeley Castle.

The vault, in the centre of the choir, seemed to be the ideal location in which to bury Charles. Richmond checked the space available and found that it was large enough to accommodate Charles's coffin. Herbert's and Mildmay's concern about the body of King Charles lying in the same vault as that of Henry VIII seems not to have concerned the Lords.

37. The Choir of St. George's Chapel.

Whilst the vault lay open and when the chapel was empty, it is reported that it was entered by a soldier who was looking for any items of value. He broke a hole in Henry's coffin but found nothing. However, he removed a piece of the velvet pall covering the coffin, which he did not think would be missed, and also a piece of bone. The soldier was caught, explaining later that he had intended to use the bone to make a handle for a knife. It is not known what punishment, if any, he received. It must be presumed that the bone and piece of pall were returned to the vault.

The lead coffin of King Charles still bore no inscription. Richmond managed to obtain a strip of soft lead some two feet long and two inches broad. On this he inscribed the words "KING CHARLES 1648". This strip was then soldered to the top of the coffin.

It is said that one of the noblemen present wished to look once more on the face of his dead master, and that the coffin was briefly opened before being sealed for the last time. This must be doubtful, as by this time the lead coffin had been sealed shut and opening and resealing it would not have been a quick or easy task. It would also not be recommended as eight days had passed since the execution of the King.

Richmond then saw Colonel Whichcot to make the arrangements for the funeral. Parliament had given Richmond permission to use whatever service he chose and he intended that Bishop Juxon, who by now was also at Windsor, should read the Service for the Dead from the Book of Common Prayer. The use of the Prayer Book had been prohibited by Parliament. Whichcot had other ideas, however, and despite being aware of Parliament's dispensation, he absolutely refused to allow the Prayer Book to be used on this occasion. Richmond protested loudly and at length, but Whichcot refused to give way. He did concede that if Bishop Juxon, "...had any exhortation to say, without the book, he should have leave..."

Meanwhile, the body of the King had been moved again and now lay in St. George's Hall. It was covered by a black velvet pall, probably the same one which had lain in readiness on the scaffold.

Shortly before three o'clock in the afternoon of 9th February, 1649, the small funeral procession set out for St. George's Chapel.

The coffin was carried on the shoulders of soldiers from the Windsor garrison. The black velvet pall covered the coffin and reached nearly to the ground on either side. The front end of the pall was turned back over the coffin to enable the bearers at the front to see their way. The rest of the pall would have hidden all the other bearers. The four corners of the pall were held by the four Lords, Richmond, Hertford, Lindsay and Southampton. Bishop Juxon followed the coffin and carried the Book of Common Prayer, which remained closed. Then followed the rest of the King's servants, who included Herbert, and finally Colonel Whichcot, who was there to make sure his specific instructions were carried out.

Although the King's children, Prince Henry and Princess Elizabeth, had been allowed to see their father just before the execution, they were not allowed to be present at the funeral.

The severely cold January weather had still not broken. It began to snow as the coffin was carried from St. George's Hall to the Chapel. The snow fell so fast that by the time the short journey to the west end of the Chapel had been completed, the black velvet pall had received a coating of white. Much was made of this at the time, for Charles had, unusually, worn white at his Coronation, rather than the more traditional purple robes and his coffin was covered in white snow, the colour of innocence, when his body entered St. George's Chapel, his final resting place.

Bishop Juxon refused to extemporise a funeral service at the graveside in the Puritan manner as Whichcot had suggested. Nothing was said, no service was heard, no prayers said aloud. The heavy coffin was lowered in silence into the vault, the silence in the chapel being disturbed only by the muffled sounds of movement amongst the small group surrounding the entrance to the vault in the floor of the choir.

After the coffin had been placed in the vault, there was a moment of hesitation over what to do with the velvet pall. Richmond indicated that it should remain over the coffin, now in the darkness of the vault.

The Lords, Bishop Juxon and the few servants and friends of the King present quietly left the Chapel. Colonel Whichcot remained to supervise

38. 19th century painting by Ernest Crofts, showing the burial of Charles I.

the resealing of the vault and the replacement of the paving slabs of the floor of the choir.

As Herbert was later to write "...So went the White King to his grave, in the forty-eighth year of his age and the twenty-second year and tenth month of his reign."

IX   REPUBLIC, RESTORATION
AND REGICIDES

The concern raised in Europe over the trial and subsequent execution of Charles I died down with surprising speed as the new Republican Government established itself in England. Statesmen abroad who had previously expressed their abhorrence at the execution of the King were, within a few years, on good political terms with the English Parliament.

The political importance of the death of the King actually grew larger with the passing of time, and not smaller as perhaps would have been expected. This was largely as a result of the conduct of the King at his trial and on the scaffold, as details of the events became better known. The fact that Charles I met his fate with purpose and resolution almost compelled respect for him and his cause.

Although the execution of the King caused great consternation in England, the most common feeling seems to have been one of stunned amazement and most people went about their usual business almost in a state of shock. One Foreign Ambassador in London commented, "There was no disturbance in London on the day of the execution; all the shops were open in the usual way."

There was a genuine grief, expressed by many. A writer in the *Kingdom's Weekly Intelligencer* said,

> "This day it did not rain at all, yet it was a very wet day in and about the City of London by reason of the abundance of affliction that fell from my eyes."

In March, 1649, Parliament passed an Act which abolished the office of King saying that

> "...the office of a King in this nation shall not henceforth reside in or be exercised by any one single person; and that no person whatsoever shall or may have, or hold the office, style, dignity, power or authority of King of the said Kingdoms and Dominions, or any of them, or of the Prince of Wales..."

In an Act establishing a Council of State and appointing the new Councillors, it was stated that they,

> "...are authorised and required to oppose and suppress whomsoever shall [support] the pretended title of Charles Stuart, eldest son of the late King, or any other of the late King's issue, or claiming under him or them the, or the pretended title or claims of any other single person whomsoever to the crown of England or Ireland, dominion of Wales or to any of the dominions or territories to them or either of them belonging."

The intention was that Parliament be re-elected, but for various reasons, including a war with the Dutch, the elections never happened. Cromwell served on several Committees and was concerned over the delayed elections, but was determined not to use force to expedite them.

In April 1653, however, Parliament tried to pass legislation which would have extended its life and effectively remove the need for elections. This time Cromwell and the Army moved swiftly and the members of Parliament were literally evicted from the Commons Chamber. "Take away that bauble!" Cromwell shouted as he hurled the Mace, symbol of Royal power, from the table.

With Parliament dissolved, Cromwell saw himself as only a temporary Steward of the affairs of the nation, until a new Parliament assembled, which it did in July of 1653. It was the intention that the new Parliament would agree a Constitution and means of effectively running the Country, but the new members were unable to agree and effectively surrendered many of their powers to Cromwell. Parliament still had power over legislation and was obliged to sit at least once every three years. Cromwell had no right of veto over legislation, as Charles had had, but he did have the authority of the Army behind him.

On 16th December 1653, Cromwell was installed as Lord Protector in a simple service held in Westminster Abbey. He had refused to accept the title of King which Parliament offered him. The nation seemed to yearn for a single figurehead, be he called King or Protector.

The new role meant Cromwell had to improve his manners and attire. He had to become used to those who had been his fellow officers removing their hats in his presence and referring to him as "Your Highness", the adopted correct form of address for the new position.

During the period of the Commonwealth, there were various plans for armed uprisings to restore Charles II to the throne, but all came to nothing. In May 1658 a Royalist plot for a rising in London went off half-cock and the leading conspirators were arrested and executed.

When England and France were engaged in a war with Spain, Charles entertained some hope that a Spanish victory would assist his cause. Charles's brother, the Duke of York actually fought in the Spanish Army; Charles himself was only prevented by his followers from doing so himself. A Spanish defeat in 1658, however, resulted in a peace treaty the following year which wiped out any Royalist hopes of aid from Spain.

On 3rd September 1658, Oliver Cromwell died and was succeeded in the position of Lord Protector by his son Richard. Charles II issued a declaration at the time that all his subjects should help to restore his royal authority and, "...resist the usurper Richard Cromwell." At the same time, however, he expressed the wish that his supporters would not do anything rash for him. Charles hoped that the Presbyterians, who hated Cromwell, might rise against the Protectorate creating a timely moment for his own supporters to join in the opposition.

In fact the death of Cromwell, surprisingly, caused very little unrest and worry. Clarendon wrote years after that,

> "...never monarch, after he had inherited a crown by many descents, died with more silence nor with less alteration; the same or a greater calm in the kingdom than had been before."

This left Charles's position desperate. In a letter to the King at the time, Clarendon (then still Hyde) wrote,

> "We have not yet found the advantage by Cromwell's death as we reasonably hoped, nay, rather we are the worse for it, and the less esteemed, people imagining by the great calm that hath followed that the nation is united and that in truth the King hath very few friends."

In January 1659, however, Parliament was summoned and contained many concealed Royalists. In Parliament the divisions between the Army and the Republican leaders were coming to a head and Richard Cromwell did not have the strength of personality to keep them under control as his father had done. The Army forced Richard Cromwell to dissolve Parliament but then realised that they had no constitution ready to replace the Protectorate and were forced to recall the remains of the 1640 Parliament. This was known as the Rump Parliament and was regarded by the Republicans as the legal government of the country.

At this time there were various plans for Charles to return to England and for there to be risings in his cause, but all came to nothing.

The new Parliament met in April 1660 and comprised many more Royalist supporters. It was clear that the Protectorate was not the favoured means of government and that the re-establishment of a monarchy, with a known and accepted constitution, but with the powers of the King and Parliament clearly defined, and Parliament's authority confirmed, seemed the preferred option. Negotiations between the King and Parliament opened in earnest.

Charles had always been agreeable to making any promises necessary to secure his position. He agreed that the officers and soldiers of the Army would be treated generously, promised liberty of conscience, and had to accept the new power and role of Parliament. Charles remained, however, constant on one point, that of demanding revenge on those directly responsible for his father's murder.

On 1st May 1660, Parliament agreed unanimously to invite Charles to return to England to be crowned King. Much popular rejoicing was to follow. On 29th May, the day of his thirtieth birthday, Charles entered Whitehall. According to those present, the way was,

> "...strewed with flowers...the bells ringing, the streets hung with tapestry, the fountains running with wine."

The Army was disbanded leaving only one regiment of infantry, which came to be known as the Coldstream Guards. Whilst in the process of being disbanded, the Army had to put down some minor demonstrations and objections to the restoration of the monarchy by committed Republicans. The soldiers finally received their arrears of pay, when Charles persuaded Parliament to foot the bill.

In the August of 1660, in accordance with Charles's wishes, Parliament passed the Act of Indemnity, which promised no reprisals for any acts committed in the period of the Civil War and Commonwealth. The Act exempted, however, all the Regicides (those responsible for the murder of the King)

> "...for their execrable treason in sentencing to death or signing the instrument for the horrid murder or being instrumental in taking away the precious life of the late sovereign Lord Charles."

Forty-nine people were named, plus the two unknown executioners of Charles I. There was a proviso that if any of the Regicides were brought to trial, a decision on their fate should be delayed until the King himself, by advice and with the consent of Parliament, should order their execution.

Of the fifty-nine signatories to the Death Warrant of Charles I in 1649, fifteen had died before the Restoration of Charles II in 1660. John Bradshaw died on 31st October 1659, Oliver Cromwell on 3rd September

1658, Henry Ireton, of the plague in Ireland, in 1651 and Thomas Pride in 1658.

On the orders of the House of Commons, the bodies of these four were ordered to be exhumed and hung on the gallows at Tyburn on 30th January 1661, the anniversary of the execution of King Charles I.

In the event, only the bodies of Bradshaw, Cromwell and Ireton were exhumed and exhibited as directed. At the end of the day the heads of the bodies were struck off and displayed on poles on the top of Westminster Hall. The bodies were cast into a pit made beneath the gallows.

The head of Cromwell was probably placed on the corner of the Hall nearest the spot where Charles I had faced his judges. It remained there exposed for many years: Samuel Pepys recorded its presence there in February 1661 and it is believed that it was still there on the eve of the Glorious Revolution of 1688. It was probably still there in 1703 when it was reported that it had been blown down in the great storm of that year and sold on the spot by a sentry to a passer-by for a shilling.

The head still survives today and its history is well documented. It passed through many hands until, in recent years, it was finally sealed in a wall cavity at Sidney Sussex College, Cambridge. The head has been subjected to many tests and is believed to be genuine.

Two other Commissioners died in the year of the Restoration and many of the others still alive fled the country.

Those who had not fled were captured, tried and imprisoned. A few were able to prove that they had tried their best to save the King and were forgiven for their actions, but most of the trials resulted in executions.

Thomas Harrison, John Cook and Hugh Peters died protesting that they would never repent of their actions, whilst others were to die "...exhibiting much penitence."

John Cook, who had been the King's prosecutor wrote to his wife shortly before his execution.

"We are not traitors, nor murderers, nor fanatics, but true Christians and good Commonwealth men, fixed and constant to the principles of sanctity, truth, justice and mercy, which the Parliament and Army declared and engaged for; and to that noble principle of preferring the universality, before a particularity, that we sought the public good and would have enfranchised the people and secured the welfare of the whole groaning creation, if the nation had not more delighted in servitude than freedom."

Most of the executions took place at Charing Cross, but following a petition from the residents of the area, who were protesting about the frequency of the executions there and the resultant disruption to their work and homes, the final executions were made at Tyburn. These included Hacker and Axtell.

The executions of the Regicides began in 1660 and lasted until 1662. Some of the executions were witnessed by King Charles II himself.

In December 1660, Parliament passed a bill ordering the anniversary of the execution of King Charles I to be observed as a day of fasting and humiliation. In 1662, the Bishop of Winchester drew up a form of service for the day which was included in the Book of Common Prayer, where it remained until 1859.

A cult of "Charles the Martyr" came into existence, which grew as reports were made of cures made to the sick by "...the application of those things distainted by his blood."

Five churches around the country were dedicated to "King Charles the Martyr": at Falmouth, Plymouth, The Peak Forest, Newham Salop and Tunbridge Wells.

Charles II was finally crowned King in Westminster Abbey on St. George's Day, April 23rd, 1661. It was the ailing Archbishop of Canterbury, William Juxon, who placed the crown on the new King's head. No-one could have had a more appropriate task, for it had been Juxon who had been with King Charles I when he was executed. Westminster Hall, the setting for the trial of Charles I was now the location for a happier occasion, a splendid Coronation banquet in honour of the new King.

X REBURIAL?

After the Restoration of King Charles II in 1660, the new King and Parliament gave some consideration to the reburial of the body of King Charles I and of the erection of a suitable monument to his memory. The grave of Charles I in St. George's Chapel remained unmarked and it was even asserted at the time that he had been buried in secret at Whitehall and that the coffin buried at Windsor was filled with bricks and other rubbish.

Lord Clarendon, in his *History of the Great Rebellion*, states that it was always the intention of Charles II to rebury Charles I and that he,

> "...spoke often of it, as if it were only deferred till some circumstances and ceremonies in the doing it might be adjusted."

No positive action was, however, taken and Clarendon continues, "...by degrees the discourse of it was diminished, as if it were totally laid aside upon some reason of state." Clarendon also explains that the reason why no action was taken was that Charles's body could not be found. He added weight to this argument by stating that after the Restoration of Charles II, two of the Lords who were present at the burial of Charles I, Southampton and Lindsay, went to Windsor with their servants, who had also been with them at the time of the burial, "...but were unable to find the spot where the King had been buried."

Clarendon says that,

> "...the confusion they had at the time observed to be in that church, all things pulled down which distinguished between the body of the church and the quire, and small alterations which were begun to be made towards decency, so totally perplexed their memories that they could not satisfy themselves in what place or part of the church the royal body was interred."

Under their directions the ground was opened in several places, but without any success, and in the end, the projected reburial was, for the moment, abandoned.

There is no reason to give any credit at all to this account. The site of the burial was, in fact, well known. Samuel Pepys recorded in his famous Diary, that he had been shown the spot on 26th February, 1666, when he visited the Chapel.

St. George's Chapel was damaged during the Civil War, but it suffered surprisingly little and certainly not to the extent that Clarendon would have us believe. There is no evidence whatsoever that the screen between the nave and the choir had been damaged or that the stalls of the choir had been damaged or replaced.

If Southampton and Lindsay had genuinely forgotten the exact place of burial, which is unlikely, they could have repeated their floor-tapping routine, which would have soon relocated the vault.

The real reason why the plans for a reburial were not pursued in earnest, at least during Clarendon's lifetime (he died in 1674) was that Charles II was suffering from a chronic lack of money, following his Parliament's failure to provide him with the income it had promised. Not being able to find the dead King's body was a very convenient excuse and no doubt Southampton and Lindsay were instructed to report that the body could not be found to prevent the King being pressed by others to rebury his father.

The matter was not, however, forgotten. On 30th January, 1678 (appropriately on the anniversary of the execution of Charles I) the House of Commons sat in Committee with Sir Philip Warwick in the chair. This Committee had been formed specifically to take in hand the reburial of Charles I. Charles II had himself calculated the cost of a reburial to be £80,000, although Secretary Williamson added that, "...if there be a monument, the charge will not presently begin, it will be four years in building."

Secretary Coventry proposed that there should be a procession and a monument and stated that it would have been done before but, "...the great charge, and the wars we have been in almost ever since the King's Restoration, have hindered the King from doing it."

A long discussion followed about the most suitable site for the reburial. St. Paul's was suggested. At this time the great Cathedral was being rebuilt, to a design of Sir Christopher Wren, following the Great Fire of London in 1666. Others suggested the Henry VII Chapel in Westminster Abbey. After all the debate, no firm decision had been made and it was left that the final choice should be at, "...the King's pleasure."

To finance the venture, it was decided that two months' tax should be levied at the rate of £34,000 each month. A Bill to this effect was ordered to be brought before the full House of Commons. On 12th February the Bill received its first and second readings in the Commons and on

20th March it was considered in Grand Committee.

The only speech recorded from the meeting of the Grand Committee was that of a Mr. Waller who stated that,

"The other day I was at Windsor, and an old Sexton showed me the place where the late King was buried in St. George's Chapel."

If we assume that the Sexton indicated the correct location, it is apparent that the site of the burial was known after all. If there were any remaining doubts in this respect, they were quickly resolved by Herbert, who was still alive and in a position to identify the exact spot. He also stated that he personally had seen the King's body laid in his coffin and was present at the burial.

Herbert was at this time in the process of writing his memoirs, which form an excellent account of the last days of Charles I. The memoirs do concentrate on Herbert's own services and actions towards Charles I and contain many small errors and incorrect dates. To be fair to Herbert, it must be remembered that by this time he was over seventy years old and was writing of events which had occurred thirty years before. It is doubtful if he had access to any contemporary news-sheets to enable him to check some of the details in his account.

39. The Wolsey Chapel, now known as the Albert Memorial Chapel: St George's Chapel, Windsor Castle.

Charles II finally decided that his father's body should remain at Windsor, but that it should be transferred into a new mausoleum which was to be designed by Sir Christopher Wren. The mausoleum was to be built on the site of Cardinal Wolsey's Chapel, which adjoined and formed part of St. George's Chapel. This particular part of the Chapel did suffer badly during the Civil War on the orders of Parliament, mainly because of the large number of religious statues with which it was decorated. The Chapel, built during the reign of Henry VIII, had never been completed and at the time of the Restoration still remained an empty shell. The new plans would have meant its complete demolition.

The designs for the new mausoleum and tomb for King Charles I were drawn up by Sir Christopher Wren in 1678. The original estimate for the work, in Wren's own hand, survives in All Souls College at Oxford.

The design for the mausoleum was for a circular building surmounted by a large dome. The dome was to be decorated with twenty large allegorical figures around the base of the drum and topped with an even larger statue of "Fame".

Both the exterior and interior of the building were to be rich in detail and covered in carved and painted decoration.

The total cost of the work was estimated at £43,663. 2s. 0d., and included the following:

For 70 rod of foundation, with digging, at £5	£350
For the shafts of 20 halfe columns, each shaft being 27 feet high..	£1,350
For 20 intercolumnes..	£760
For 20 half capitals, at £35 each stone and work	£700
For 20 festoons with the stones of the intercolumnes between the capitells, at £16 each	£320
For 240 feet running of cornice, 3 foot projecting with modillions and ornaments..	£840
For 20 figures of the great life	£2,000
For a large figure of brasse, gilt, on the top, being 10 foot high	£1,000
For 4,260 foot superficial of stucco, and the best paint in fresco, in the spandrills between windowes and in ye cupolo, at 10s ye foot.	£2,310
For a brass dore	£50
For a marble dore in the vaults	£20

For the tomb itself, Wren estimated:

For 10 figures of the great life, cut in brasse and gilt, at £500 figure	£5,000
For 7 children of brass gilt, each £200, with ornaments belonging	£1,400
For the pedestal of touch, and the steps of rich marble and other appertenances	£300
A gratuity for an excellent statuary, for his skill in moulding and founding, over and above the value of the worke	£1,500

SUMMARY

First story without	£11,669 00 00
Second story without	£5,092 02 00
Brick work within	£1,225 00 00
Ornaments of the first story within	£11,032 00 00
Ornaments within the cupola	£6,445 00 00
The monument itself	£8,200 00 00
Total Charges	*£43,663 02 00*

The plans for the tomb itself, also detailed by Wren, were:

"In the Middle-niche fronting the entrance, was designed Kings Monument, after this manner. Four statues, Emblems of heroick Virtues, standing on a square Basis, or Plinth, and pressing underneath, prostrate Figures of Rebellion, Heresy, Hypocrisy, Envy &c. support a large Shield, on which is a Statue erect of the *royal Martyr*, in modern Armour, over his head is a Group of Cherubims, bearing a Crown, branches of Palm and other devices. There are two Draughts of this Statuary Design, (By the eminent Artificer, Mr. Gibbons) one adapted for Brass-work, the other for Marble, as should have been most approved."

The design included other niches around the interior of the building, which would have been available for other tombs. Perhaps it was the intention of Charles II that the mausoleum for his father should also become his own final resting-place and that of his successors, and/or of other members of the royal family, or of notable people who had supported the cause of his father.

Had the mausoleum been completed, it would have undoubtedly been a most impressive building, if perhaps, to modern eyes, an incongruous addition to the Gothic architectural style of St. George's Chapel

40. Drawing by Sir Christopher Wren of the planned mausoleum for Charles I at Windsor.

and the setting of Windsor Castle. With the finest architect and designs and using the best craftsmen available, the mausoleum would have been a splendid example of the English Baroque style and possibly one of Wren's finest achievements after St. Paul's Cathedral in London.

The Bill to approve the plans was prepared for Parliament, but on 15th July, 1678, Parliament was prorogued and was not to meet again until 21st October. In the intervening period the "Popish Plot" was discovered and all thoughts of a mausoleum and tomb for Charles I were forgotten. Parliament and the King struggled over the renewed persecution of Catholics and the introduction of the Bill of Exclusion, which was an attempt by Parliament to prevent the Catholic James, Duke of York, and next in line to the throne, from succeeding Charles II.

Charles was to assemble and dissolve Parliament several times in the following years. The last Parliament of his reign met in March 1681, but for the last four years of his reign he managed without Parliament. This shows, perhaps, that Charles II was better able to deal with a rebellious Parliament than had been his father. All this meant that the Bill to rebury Charles was never actually presented to Parliament, and that the monies needed were never raised. Charles II was, therefore, unable to honour his dead father as he may have wished.

Upon the death of Charles II in 1685, despite the efforts of Parliament to exclude him from the throne, Charles's brother James became King as James II. There are no records that James, the second son of Charles I, ever considered the reburial of his father. His short reign was beset with other problems and was only to last for three years, when in 1688, after the bloodless "Glorious Revolution", his daughter Mary and her Dutch husband, William of Orange, became, at the request of Parliament, joint sovereigns. It is doubtful if either Mary, or later Queen Anne, ever considered the reburial of their grandfather. By this time, almost all those who had fought with or against the King and those who had witnessed his execution were themselves dead.

Charles I still lay in an unmarked grave.

XI   1649 TO 1813

Whilst all the debates and discussions about a possible reburial of the body of King Charles I were taking place, the small vault in St. George's Chapel remained undisturbed.

During the short reign of James II (1685-1688) the floor of the choir was repaved. The original floor had become worn through centuries of use and the new floor was of hard-wearing slabs of black and white marble, laid in alternate squares. This is the floor we see today in the Chapel. The work of laying the floor must to some extent have disturbed the vault, the roof of which lay immediately below the paving. Surprisingly, the opportunity was not taken to mark the site of the vault.

In 1696, the vault was reopened for another royal burial, this time for a stillborn child of the Princess George of Denmark (Anne, daughter of James II and later to be Queen Anne). The birth must have occurred at Windsor and this vault was probably the most convenient place for the burial to be made. Space in the vault was limited and rather than place the tiny coffin on the floor of the vault, it was laid on King Charles's coffin.

It is interesting that this particular vault was used, bearing in mind the discussions about the location of the vault years before. The exact site of the vault may well have been rediscovered when the floor of the Chapel was relaid, even if the knowledge about the occupants had been forgotten.

By the reign of George III (1760-1820) Windsor had become one of the royal family's favourite palaces. George III decided to arrange for the building of a new burial vault in St. George's Chapel for the use of his family. He chose as the site for the vault the area beneath the large Chapel known as "Wolsey's Chapel". It was this Chapel which had been earmarked for demolition when plans for a new mausoleum for Charles I were first raised. The Chapel remained unfinished. Cardinal Wolsey had intended to be buried in this Chapel during the reign of Henry VIII, but this was not to be. Henry too had plans to be buried there, but he was buried in a small vault beneath the choir.

At the start of the nineteenth century, the Chapel was still an empty shell. The construction of the new vault also saw the Chapel completed. The vault, beneath the floor of the Chapel, was designed to accommodate forty-eight coffins and was later to hold a number of important royal burials, which included George III, George IV and William IV. The Chapel became known as the "Tomb House". Today we know it as the Albert Memorial Chapel, because of the splendid memorial it contains to Prince Albert, consort of Queen Victoria.

Access to this vault is now from behind the high altar, but when first constructed the entrance was through the floor of the choir. When a burial in this vault was made, the coffin would be lowered into a small chamber beneath the floor of the main Chapel, where a passage connected to the vault beneath Wolsey's Chapel.

There is a large amount of space available beneath the floor of St. George's Chapel and it holds many burial vaults constructed over the centuries. Early in 1813, the Duchess of Brunswick (the mother of the Princess of Wales) died, and preparations were put in hand for her burial in a small vault beneath the floor of the choir, a vault which must be adjacent to the old royal vault. The work in opening this vault for the burial, together with the other work in hand in the construction of the new royal vault, all meant that there was a great deal of excavation being undertaken in the area of the choir.

During the course of all this building work, in March 1813, the workmen accidentally broke through the brick wall of the old vault. The builders may have been aware of the likelihood of encountering other vaults in the area, but their precise location may have been forgotten. Looking through the hole in the wall, the workmen were able to see three coffins. The largest coffin was assumed to be that of Henry VIII and the second coffin to be that of Jane Seymour. From the known accounts of the burial of Charles I, the third coffin, still covered by a black velvet pall, was identified as being that of Charles I.

The Prince Regent, later to become King George IV, was notified immediately that a royal burial had been disturbed. At the instigation of the Prince an examination of the vault was made and it was decided that the coffin, which was presumed to be that of King Charles I, should be opened.

A full account of the opening of the coffin was made by Sir Henry Halford, personal Physician to the Prince Regent. Halford's presence at the examination was obviously necessary to deal professionally with the opening of the coffin and to report on the findings from a medical viewpoint.

Sir Henry was a fellow of the Royal College of Physicians, and was later to become its President from 1820 to 1844. He published his account which appeared in *The Examiner* of 11th April, 1813 and also in the *Annual Register* for 1813. The account was later reprinted, along with other items, in a volume entitled *Essays and Orations* which was published in 1831 and reprinted in 1833.

41. The Prince Regent, later George IV. Portrait, dated 1814, by Sir Thomas Lawrence.

42. Sir Henry Halford. Portrait, dated 1809, by Sir William Beechey.

The account caused a great deal of interest at the time and was widely reported and quoted in the press.

The Times of 7th April, 1813 gave a provisional account of the examination and ends,

> "...we understand that by the command of the Prince Regent, a full account of this interesting discovery, as far as it regards the martyred King, is to be prepared by Sir Henry Halford."

Interest was aroused and *The Times* also printed a short article on the burial of King Charles I in its edition of 17th April. On 28th April, *The Times* printed a larger extract from Halford's account. The opening of the vault was also the subject of the satirical cartoonists of the day, who fully exploited the idea of the Prince Regent examining the mortal remains of one of his predecessors.

Halford's account is short, but remarkably precise. As he states, his intention was to "...record the facts only, and not opinions." He could not, however, refrain from expressing some opinions. In the light of more recent and accurate information, he has been proved to be incorrect in only minor points.

The next chapter quotes Halford's account in full. The words are his, and his original punctuation and spelling are retained.

XII   EXHUMATION

"AN ACCOUNT of what appeared on OPENING THE COFFIN of KING CHARLES THE FIRST, in the vault of King Henry VIII, in ST. GEORGE'S CHAPEL, WINDSOR, on the first of April MDCCCXIII.

It is stated by Lord Clarendon, in his History of the Rebellion, that the body of King Charles I., though known to be interred in St. George's Chapel, at Windsor, could not be found, when searched for there some years afterwards. It seems, by the historian's account, to have been the wish and the intention of King Charles II., after his restoration, to take up his father's corpse, and to reinter it in Westminster Abbey, with those royal honours which it had been denied it under the government of the regicides. The most careful search was made for the body by several people, amongst whom were some of those noble persons whose faithful attachment had led them to pay their last tribute of respect to their unfortunate master by attending him to the grave. Yet such had been the injury done to the chapel, such were the mutilations it had undergone, during the period of the userpation, that no marks were left, by which the EXACT place of burial of the king could be ascertained. [Pope, alluding to the doubt which was entailed in his day, as to the place of the King's interment, invokes the Muse to,

'Make sacred Charles's tomb for ever known,
(Obscure the place and uninscribed the stone)'

'Windsor Forest', v. 319].

There is some difficulty in reconciling this account with the information which has reached us since the death of Lord Clarendon, particularly with that of Mr. Ashmole, and more especially with the most interesting narrative of Mr. Herbert, given in the "Athenae Oxonienses". Mr. Herbert had been a groom of the bed-chamber, and a faithful companion of the king in all circumstances, from the time he left the Isle of Wight, until his death - was employed to convey his body to Windsor, and to fix upon a proper place for his interment there; and was an eye-witness to that interment, in the vault of King Henry VIII.

Were it allowable to hazard a conjecture, after Lord Clarendon's deprecation of all conjectures on the subject, one might suppose that it was deemed imprudent, by the ministers of King Charles II. that his Majesty should indulge his pious inclination to re-inter his father, at a period when those ill-judged effusions of loyalty which had been manifested by taking out of the graves and hanging up the bodies of some of the most active members of the court which had condemned and executed the king might, in the event of another triumph of the republicans, have subjected the body of the monarch to similar indignity. But the fact is, King Charles I. was buried in the vault of King Henry VIII. situated precisely where Mr. Herbert has described it; and an accident has served to elucidate a point of history, which the great authority of Lord Clarendon had involved in some obscurity.

(Mr. Herbert, whose account furnished the clue to our enquiry, retired immediately after his Majesty's death into Yorkshire, and lived until the beginning of the next century. His papers were not published until some time after his death).

On completing the mausoleum which his present Majesty has built in the tomb-house, as it is called, it was necessary to form a passage to it from under the choir of St. George's Chapel. In constructing this passage, an aperture was made accidentally in one of the walls of the vault of King Henry VIII., through which the workmen were able to see, not only the two coffins, which were supposed to contain the bodies of King Henry VIII. and Queen Jane Seymour, but a third also, covered with a black velvet pall, which, from Mr. Herbert's narrative, might fairly be presumed to hold the remains of King Charles I.

On representing the circumstances to the Prince Regent, his Royal Highness perceived at once, that a doubtful point in history might be cleared by opening this vault; and accordingly his Royal Highness ordered an examination to be made on the first convenient opportunity. This was done on the first of April last, the day after the funeral of the Duchess of Brunswick, in the presence of his Royal Highness himself, who guaranteed thereby the most respectful care and attention to the remains of the dead during the enquiry. His Royal Highness was accompanied by His Royal Highness the Duke of Cumberland, Count Munster, the Dean of Windsor, Benjamin Charles Stevenson, Esq., and Sir Henry Halford.

The vault is covered by an arch, half a brick in thickness, is seven feet two inches in width, nine feet six inches in length, and four feet ten inches in height, and is situated in the centre of the choir, opposite the eleventh knight's stall, on the sovereign's side.

On removing the pall, a plain leaden coffin, with no appearance of ever having been enclosed in wood, and bearing an inscription 'KING CHARLES, 1648', in large, legible characters, on a scroll of lead encircling it, immediately presented itself to the view. A square opening was then made in the upper part of the lid, of such dimensions as to admit a clear insight into its contents. These were, an internal wooden coffin, very much decayed, and the body carefully wrapped up in cere-cloth, into the folds of which a quantity of unctuous or greasy matter mixed with resin, as it seemed, had been melted, so as to exclude, as effectually as possible, the external air. The coffin was completely full; and from the tenacity of the cere-cloth, great difficulty was experienced in detaching it successfully from the parts which it enveloped. Wherever the unctuous matter had insinuated itself, the separation of the cere-cloth was easy; and when it came off, a correct impression of the features to which it had been applied was observed in the unctuous substance. At length, the whole of the face was disengaged from its covering. The complexion of the skin of it was dark and discoloured. The forehead and temples had lost little or nothing of their muscular substance; the cartilage of the nose was gone; but the left eye, in the first moment of exposure, was open and full, though it vanished almost immediately: and the pointed beard, so characteristic of the period of the reign of King Charles, was perfect. The shape of the face was a long oval; many of the teeth remained; and the left ear, in the consequence of the interposition of the unctuous matter between it and the cere-cloth, was found entire.

It was difficult, at this moment, to withhold a declaration, that, notwithstanding its disfigurement, the countenance did bear a strong resemblance to the coins, the busts, and especially to the pictures of King Charles I. by Vandyke, by which it had been made familiar to us. It is true, that the minds of the spectators of this interesting sight were well prepared to receive this impression; but it is also certain, that such a facility of belief had been occasioned by the simplicity and truth of Mr. Herbert's Narrative, every part of which had been confirmed by the investigation, so far as it had advanced: and it will not be denied that the shape of the face, the forehead, an eye, and the beard, are the most important features by which resemblance is determined.

When the head had been entirely disengaged from the attachments which confined it, it was found to be loose, and, without difficulty, was taken up and held to view. It was quite wet, and gave a greenish red tinge to paper and linen which touched it. (I have not asserted this liquid to be blood, because I had not an opportunity of being sure that it was so, and I wished to record facts only, and not opinions: I believe it, however, to have been blood, in which the head rested. It gave to writing paper, and to a white handkerchief, such a colour as blood which has been kept for a length of time generally leaves behind it. Nobody present had a doubt of its being blood; and it appears from Mr. Herbert's narrative, that the King was embalmed immediately after decapitation. It is probable, therefore, that the large blood vessels continued to empty themselves for some time afterwards. I am aware, that some softer parts of the human body, and particularly the brain, undergo, in the course of time, a decomposition, and will melt. A liquid, therefore, might be found long after interment, where solids only had been buried: but the weight of the head, in this instance, gave no suspicion that the brain had lost its substance; and no moisture appeared in any other part of the coffin, as far as we could see, excepting at the back of the head and neck).

The back part of the scalp was entirely perfect, and had a remarkably fresh appearance; the pores of the skin being more distinct, as they usually are when soaked in moisture; and the tendons and ligaments of the neck were of considerable substance and firmness. The hair was thick at the back part of the head, and, in appearance, nearly black. A portion of it, which has since been cleaned and dried, is of a beautiful dark brown colour. That of the beard was a redder brown. On the back part of the head it was more than an inch in length, and had probably been cut so short for the convenience of the executioner, or perhaps by the piety of friends soon after death, in order to furnish memorials of the unhappy king.

On holding up the head, to examine the place of separation from the body, the muscles of the neck had evidently retracted themselves considerably; and the fourth cervical vertebra was found to be cut through its substance transversely, leaving the surfaces of the divided portions perfectly smooth and even, an appearance which could have been produced only with a heavy blow, inflicted with a very sharp instrument, and which furnished the last proof wanting to identify King Charles the First.

After this examination of the head, which served every purpose in view, and without examining the body below the neck, it was

43. Halford's drawing of the head of Charles I.

immediately restored to its situation, the coffin was soldered up again, and the vault closed.

Neither of the other coffins had any inscription upon them. The larger one, supposed on good grounds to contain the remains of King Henry VIII. measured six feet ten inches in length, and had been enclosed in an elm one of two inches in thickness: but this was decayed, and lay in small fragments near it. The leaden coffin appeared to have been beaten in by violence about the middle; and a considerable opening in that part of it exposed a mere skeleton of the king. Some beard remained on the chin, but there was nothing to discriminate the personage contained in it.

The smaller coffin, understood to be that of Queen Jane Seymour, was not touched; mere curiosity not being considered, by the Prince Regent, as a sufficient motive for disturbing these remains.

On examining the vault with some attention, it was found that the wall, at the west end, had, at some period or other, been partly pulled down and repaired again, not by regular masonry, but by fragments of stones and bricks, put rudely and hastily together without cement. From Lord Clarendon's account, as well as from Mr. Herbert's narrative of the interment of King Charles, it is to be inferred, that the ceremony was a very hasty one, performed in the presence of the Governor, who had refused to allow the service according to the Book of Common Prayer to be used on the occasion; and had, probably, scarcely admitted the time necessary for a decent deposit of the body. It is not unlikely, therefore, that the coffin of King Henry VIII. had been injured by a precipitate introduction of the coffin of King Charles; and that the Governor was not under the influence of feelings, in those times, which gave him any concern about the Royal remains, or the vault which contained them.

It may be right to add, that a very small mahogany coffin, covered with crimson velvet, containing the body of an infant, had been laid upon the pall which covered King Charles. This is known to have been a still-born child of the Princess George of Denmark, afterwards Queen Anne.

LONDON, APRIL 11, 1813.   Sir HENRY HALFORD, Bart., M.D., G.H.C.

AUTHENTICATION. When the manuscript containing the above account was read to his Royal Highness, the Prince Regent, by whose command it had been drawn up, his Royal Highness was pleased to desire that He might authenticate it, which He did immediately previous to its being deposited in the British Museum."

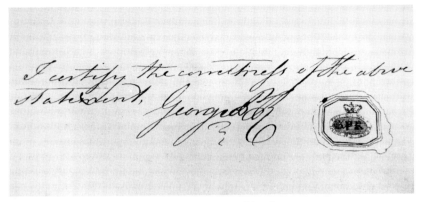

44. The authentication of the Prince Regent.

From the account of the burial of Charles I, many of the observations made by Halford agree with the known facts. A few areas of Halford's account are worthy of further comment.

Halford clearly states that there was no evidence of any external wooden coffin. Had such a coffin ever existed, parts of it would have been preserved, albeit in a fragmentary condition. The velvet pall still covered the coffin and must, therefore, still have been in a reasonable state of preservation, which indicates that wood would also have survived in the vault. Halford specifically mentions the very decayed outer coffin of Henry VIII. In mentioning the damage to Henry's coffin, Halford implies that it may have been damaged by the careless lowering of the coffin of Charles I into the small vault. This is possible, but it is likely that the damage was inflicted by the soldier, mentioned earlier.

The description of the head of Charles I is very precise. Mr. Julian Litten, of the Victoria and Albert Museum in London and Dr. A.C. Hunt, a Home Office Consultant Pathologist, have both been able to confirm that the appearance of the head is what would be expected from a body which had been enclosed in a lead coffin for some time. Many lead coffins have been opened in more recent times and exhibit the same characteristics as described by Halford.

Dr. Hunt has described the head of a middle-aged woman, buried in a lead coffin in the Church Yard of St. Marylebone Parish Church, about one hundred and fifty years ago. The cartilage of her nose had disappeared. The pores of her skin were very prominent and her eyebrows were well preserved, which suggests that a beard would have been similarly well preserved. Dr. Hunt states that it is his experience that in bodies buried in lead coffins, the muscles and tendons ("the tendons and filaments") of the neck are often well preserved, as described by Halford.

Halford mentions that one eye vanished immediately. Dr. Hunt points out that this is a possibility, but that it is an "old wive's tale" that bodies crumble to dust as soon as the air reaches them. What really happens is that the body, or parts of it, may be so extremely fragile, that the slightest disturbance or touch makes them fall apart.

In the course of his work, Dr. Hunt has seen the cervical vertebra of one person who had been judicially decapitated in the past, and he too remarked on the perfectly smooth and even surfaces of the cut ends. The fourth cervical vertebra is, incidentally, the most likely vertebra to be severed in such a judicial decapitation.

Halford has his own theory as to why the King's hair had been cut so short. It is clear from the accounts of the execution that Charles's hair was not cut by the Headsman and it is unlikely that it was cut by "pious friends" to provide mementoes of the King.

From the account of the embalming of the body of the King, we know that his severed head was sewn back on. Halford states that the head was removed from the coffin "without difficulty", which must have meant that the stitches had rotted with the passing of time.

The temptation to examine the body further, and also to examine the other coffins in the vault in more detail, must have been great but, as Halford stated, mere curiosity was not considered a sufficient motive to disturb the bodies further. The Prince Regent had set out to resolve a "doubtful point in history" and with that task accomplished, it was his wish that the occupants of that small vault be disturbed no more and that the bodies of the two Kings, one Queen and one child, be left in peace.

Soon after the exhumation, many cartoons appeared in the press. The one included here is typical and is dated May 1813.

In this cartoon, the Prince Regent says,

"Aye, There's great Harry! - Great indeed!! for he got rid of many wives, whilst I, poor soul can't get rid of one...Cut of his beard Doctor t'will make me a prime pair of Royal Whiskers!!"

The Prince Regent at this time was undergoing a difficult relationship with his wife, Caroline of Brunswick.

45. Contemporary cartoon by George Cruikshank,
showing the Prince Regent and Sir Henry Halford in the vault.

Another figure in the cartoon says

"How queer King Charley looks without his Head doesn't he?!! Faith
& Sure & I wonder how we should look without our Heads?!!",

a reference to the relatively recent French Revolution, which had seen the
executions of the French Royal family and many of the French Court.

It was finally left to King William IV to mark the burial place of King Charles I in St. George's Chapel.

In 1837, a memorial stone of black marble was laid in the floor of the choir, directly above the burial vault. The inscription reads:

IN A VAULT
BENEATH THIS MARBLE SLAB
ARE DEPOSITED THE REMAINS
OF
JANE SEYMOUR, QUEEN OF KING HENRY VIII
1537
KING HENRY VIII
1547
KING CHARLES I
1648
AND
AN INFANT CHILD OF QUEEN ANNE
THIS MEMORIAL WAS PLACED HERE
BY COMMAND OF
KING WILLIAM IV, 1837

After nearly two hundred years, Charles I at last lay in a marked grave. Exactly why William IV decided to have the site marked may never be known. It is interesting to note that the inscription was placed over the vault in the year of the three hundredth anniversary of the death of Jane Seymour, but this may be pure coincidence.

It may well be that William IV's predecessor, King George IV had intended to mark the spot, for as Prince Regent, it was he who was responsible for the opening of the coffin of King Charles I in 1813.

St. George's Chapel was the scene of further building activity in the reign of Queen Victoria when a new mausoleum was constructed. It was situated at Frogmore, some distance from the chapel, but it needed a passageway linking the choir of St. George's Chapel to the new vaults. The vault containing King Charles was disturbed in 1861, when the old vault

IN A VAULT
BENEATH THIS MARBLE SLAB
ARE DEPOSITED THE REMAINS
OF
JANE SEYMOUR QUEEN OF KING HENRY VIII
1537.
KING HENRY VIII.
1547.
KING CHARLES I.
1648.
AND
AN INFANT CHILD OF QUEEN ANNE.

THIS MEMORIAL WAS PLACED HERE
BY COMMAND OF
KING WILLIAM IV. 1837.

46. The memorial stone over the vault containing the body of Charles I.

was again accidentally broken into in the course of building work in the Chapel.

Returning to Halford's account of the opening of the vault in 1813, it is clear that some items were removed. Part of the beard, some hair from the back of Charles's head, part of a neck vertebra and a tooth were removed. Halford states that the hair was, "...since cleaned and dried," which must have been after the coffin and vault had been resealed.

These relics were removed quite openly by Halford and with the full consent of the Prince Regent, the Dean and the others present at the time. The piece of beard was wrapped up in a piece of Deanery writing paper, supplied by the Dean. Halford cleaned and dried the hair and studied the other items before he completed the account of the opening of the coffin. These relics were eventually taken to Halford's home, Wistow Hall, some six miles form Leicester, where they remained.

In 1888, a minor public outcry arose in the Press over the retention of these relics by Halford's family. During the seventy-five years the relics were at Wistow, they were treated with all due reverence, and were occasionally shown privately to friends, without any suggestion of impropriety.

It is clear that some misunderstanding may well have arisen among people to whom the true details of the opening of the vault in 1813 were imperfectly known. It was, no doubt, considered improper by some that such important royal relics should be allowed to be exhibited as mere curiosities, and the royal family seems to have expressed, albeit in private, some concern over this.

At this time, Sir Henry St. John Halford, grandson of Sir Henry Halford, was himself worried about the future of the relics. This was partly because of the public interest at the time, but mainly as he had no heirs, apart from a brother, who like him had no children. Sir Henry was probably concerned that the relics might be placed on the open market for sale or that they might otherwise come into the ownership of someone much less sensitive about their exhibition.

Sir Henry decided to present the relics to the Prince of Wales (later Edward VII). It is not known if it was the intention of Sir Henry that the relics should be returned to the vault at Windsor.

The casket containing the relics was handed to the Prince of Wales at Marlborough House. Lord Cottesloe, in a memorandum about the relics, tells of a "cool reception" given to Sir Henry by the Prince.

This "cool reception" from the Prince was probably because the problem of what to actually do with the relics had now shifted from Sir Henry to him. On 11th December, 1888, the Prince informed the then Dean of Windsor that he had received the relics from Sir Henry St. John

Halford, and that he had decided that they should be returned to the vault in which Charles I was buried. The Prince had already obtained the consent of Queen Victoria for the royal vault to be opened.

A full handwritten account of the replacement of the relics in the royal vault was made at the time and placed in the Royal Library at Windsor with a copy of the 1813 account of the exhumation. This 1888 account has never been published in full and includes drawings and plans of the vault. It is quoted below in its entirety.

"REPLACING OF RELICS

in

THE GRAVE OF CHARLES I

On Tuesday, Dec. 11. 1888, the Prince of Wales, then on a visit to the Queen at Windsor Castle, sent for the Dean of Windsor and showed him a small ebony casket about which His Royal Highness had previously spoken both to him and Canon Dalton.

The casket, which measured $4\frac{3}{4}$ inches in length, $3\frac{3}{4}$ inches in width, and $2\frac{1}{4}$ inches in depth, contained certain relics believed to be part of the body of King Charles I. The coffin of that King was opened for inspection by Sir Henry Halford and others in the year 1813, as recounted in Sir Henry Halford's published memorandum of the circumstances.

It would seem probable, or certain, though it is not mentioned in the published memorandum referred to, that Sir Henry Halford on that occasion removed from the King's coffin certain articles, namely (1) a portion of the cervical vertebra cut transversely with some sharp instrument, (2) a portion of the beard of the King, of auburn colour, with a bit of linen cerecloth attaching to it, (3) a tooth. These relics had come into the possession of Sir Henry Halford's grandson, Sir Henry St. John Halford, and were by him presented to the Prince of Wales in a small ebony box. The box contained the following inscription engraved on a plate inside the lid:

EN

CAROLI Imi REGIS

IPSISSIMIUM OS CERVICIS

FERRO EHEU INTERCISCUM

1648

ET REGIAM INSUPER BARBAM*

47. The Prince of Wales (later Edward VII). Photograph by Lafayette taken in the 1880s.

The portion of beard and the tooth were enclosed in a piece of stained and folded writing paper addressed "The Hon. and Most Reverend The Dean of Windsor", which would seem to show that Dean Legge had in 1813 known of this abstraction of the relics and had furnished a piece of paper at the moment in which to wrap the beard and tooth.

The Prince of Wales told the Dean that it was his wish to replace these relics in the vault or grave from which they had been abstracted. The Queen's consent having been obtained, it was arranged that the relics should be so replaced by his Royal Highness on the following Thursday, Dec. 13th.

On the evening of Tuesday, Dec. 11th, the Prince of Wales came to the Deanery and handed the Dean the ebony casket, in which His Royal Highness placed an autographed memorandum in the following terms:

> These relics of King Charles I, are deposited by Albert Edward, Prince of Wales, in the vault containing the coffin of the King, on December 13, 1888

In the meantime the Dean of Windsor had a leaden casket prepared, 10 inches long, 4 inches high, and 5 inches wide. On the lid of this leaden casket the following inscription was engraved:

> The relics enclosed in this case were taken from the coffin of King Charles I on April 1st, 1813, by Sir Henry Halford, Physician to King George III. They were by his grandson, Sir Henry St. John Halford, given to H.R.H. Albert Edward, Prince of Wales. On December 13th, 1888, they were replaced by H.R.H. in this vault, their original resting place.

This casket was again enclosed in a stout oaken case fitting closely. The small ebony box containing the relics was carefully deposited by the Dean within the leaden casket, and the oaken case containing all was firmly closed with screws.

On Thursday evening, Dec. 13, at 6 o'clock, after the close of evening service, the Dean of Windsor, with Canon Eliot (as Canon in Residence) and Canon Dalton, superintended the removal of the pavement stones above the vault. This was done with the utmost care and reverence by Mr. A.Y. Nutt (Surveyor to the Dean and Canons) and three workmen and occupied a very short time.

The vault is in the centre of the Chapel 'midway between the

Sovran's stall and the High Altar', at the fourth bay from either end of the seven bays of the choir. Six of the small squares of black and white marble were raised on the south side of the pavement in this portion of the choir; and then the mortar that lay between them and the brick arch of the vault was removed. From this about 20 bricks (each 9 inches by 3) were then taken out with the greatest care, so that no debris should fall on the coffin beneath. By this means an aperture of about 18 inches square was produced, immediately over the centre of King Charles's coffin. Looking down through this, it was possible, by the help of a light lowered into the vault, to see every corner of it quite clearly.

Comparing the measurements formerly made with those which were taken on this occasion, the dimensions of the vault seem to be as follows:- The length of the interior is 9ft 1 inch; the breadth 7ft 6 inches; and the depth from the corner of the arch to the floor line, 4ft 2 inches, and to the spring of the arch at the sides about 3ft. The lower part of the sides of the vault, to the height of about 2ft from the floor, had been at some time stained with some dark substance. The four royal coffins it now contains occupy the same position in which they are represented in the sketch made in 1861, when the eastern end of the vault became exposed during certain structural works then undertaken in connection with the passage that leads beneath the choir pavement, on under the altar, into the larger Royal Vault of George III and his descendants, which that Monarch excavated beneath the "Wolsey" or present "Memorial Chapel".

The western end of the vault is now crossed by a wooden beam about 18 inches above the coffins and about two feet from the wall at that end, and on it a brick had been left lying by the workmen on some previous occasion. The centre of the west wall of the vault shows signs of having been roughly rebuilt at some period; it looks as if the entrance to the vault had originally been constructed at that end. The Queen's coffin may have been introduced by a door there. King Henry's was lowered from above according to the description of his funeral; and King Charles's could hardly have been introduced that way, for such entrance would have been blocked by King Henry's coffin. There is now a distance of about two feet between the crown of the vault arch and the upper surface of the coffins. The large leaden coffin of King Henry VIII lies in the centre. It is in a condition of great dilapidation. The King's skull, with its very broad frontal, his thigh bones, ribs, and other portions of skeleton, are exposed to view, as the lead has been extensively ripped open, apparently, to judge by the fractured edges, owing to the action of internal force outward. The

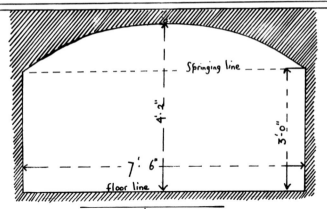

Floor line of Choir

Springing line

4' 2"

3' 0"

7' 6"

floor line

Transverse Section of Vault ∴

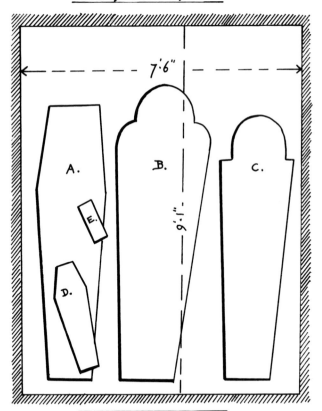

7'6"

A.

B.

C.

E.

D.

9' 1"

W
S — N
E

Plan of Vault & Coffins ⟡

48. Section and plan of the vault.

fragments of the exterior coffin, of some reddish coloured wood, about two inches in thickness, lie strewn around and upon the torn lead.

On the north side of Henry VIII, about 15 inches from him, lies the much smaller leaden coffin of Queen Jane Seymour. It is in good preservation and intact. But the wooden coffin, if there was one, that originally enclosed it, has decayed and fallen away; the wooden trestle on which the coffin rested is lying in pieces beneath it.

On the south side of Henry VIII's coffin, with a space of about three inches between their shoulders, lies that of King Charles I, covered still with a black velvet pall, which seemed to be in good preservation. This was not however raised or interfered with; but the form of the "martyr's" coffin beneath it is distinct; and therefore it would appear that the coffin containing his Majesty's remains is now in good preservation. The surface of the coffin is entirely hidden by the pall; a band of lead, with the date 1648 cut through it had been, at some previous period, drawn out from under the pall, and now rests over King Henry VIII's remains.

Upon the coffin of King Charles, near the foot, lies the small black cloth covered coffin that contains the remains of Queen Anne's infant child.

The coffin of Queen Jane Seymour is shaped round at the head and square at the shoulders; thus

That of King Henry VIII is also round at the head, and round also at the shoulders, thus

The coffin of King Charles I is of the usual plain oblong shape. All three coffins taper towards the feet; and that of King Charles I also towards the head from the shoulders.

On the present occasion, the workmen retired from the Chapel as soon as the aperture above described had been made.

The Prince of Wales came *alone* to the Chapel soon after 7pm. and in the presence of the Dean of Windsor, Canon Eliot (as canon in Residence), Canon Dalton, and Mr. A.Y. Nutt, His Royal Highness lowered the box containing the box above referred to, containing the relics, down through the aperture, and placed them carefully about the centre of King Charles's coffin.

When the Prince had retired the workmen came back again into the Chapel, and the aperture into the vault was at once re-closed. The opening in the brick arch was re-built from above, each brick being held in place by hand till the mortar had set. The marble pavement was then re-laid. The whole operation was completed by 9.30pm.

From the beginning to the end of what was done, everything was personally superintended by the Dean, Canon Eliot (canon in residence) and Canon Dalton, who remained by the side of the grave throughout. The utmost decorum and reverence was observed by the workmen. No one entered the vault."

*Translated: "See the very neck bone of King Charles I, alas cut off by iron [a sword?] 1648; and in addition, the Royal Beard."

Another brief account of these events was made by Richard Cope, Chapter Clerk in St. George's Chapel. It is dated 13th December 1888, and notes the timing of the event "Hours 6 to 10 pm."

Cope lists those present, but does not include himself, the implication being that he was present in the Chapel, but not perhaps in the immediate vicinity of the vault. Interestingly, he includes an additional name, that of Sir J.C. Cowell. He also names the three workmen as "Platt, Maltingley & Plumridge."

Cope states that "...There was no descent but the vault was examined by the eyes." He describes the casket containing the relics being "lowered/dropped into the vault be means of Mr. Nutt's handkerchief by the Prince lying on the floor." This slightly less than dignified part of the event was omitted from the official account. Cope also recorded that, "Canon Dalton's idea was that Henry VIII's coffin had been burst by the gasses evolved by the corpse."

Intriguingly, Cope makes the comment that, "Her Majesty [Queen Victoria] opposed the opening strongly at first. What arguments prevailed I did not hear."

The drawing of the interior of the vault, made at the time by Mr. A.Y. Nutt, shows the lead strip, bearing the inscription, "King Charles 1648", replaced on Charles's coffin, although the official account omits reference

49. Drawing of the interior of the vault

to this. Cope recorded that it was Nutt who removed the strip from the coffin of King Henry VIII where it had been placed in 1813 and replaced it on Charles's coffin, on top of the velvet pall, which he did not disturb. It was Mr. Nutt who produced the plan and elevation of the vault and the drawing, in sepia, of the interior of the vault. Presumably it was he who also measured the vault. His dimensions differ significantly from those recorded at the 1813 opening of the vault:

1813/1888 measurements:

Length of the vault	9ft. 6in./9ft. 1in.
Width of the vault	7ft. 2in./7ft. 6in
Height of the vault	4ft. 10in./4ft. 2in.

The 1813 measurements were taken by those who actually entered the vault, whilst in 1888 the vault was not entered. Exactly whose measurements are the most accurate will probably now never be known.

The two recorded openings of the vault have revealed many alterations made to it over the centuries. It may have been made even before it was used for the burial of King Henry VIII. The presence of apparent staining to the lower parts of the walls and floors is unusual. It may be that the walls were originally painted with pitch, or perhaps water has entered the vault at some date in the past. This might account for the extremely decayed state of the external wooden coffin of King Henry VIII. A wooden coffin in a dry and sealed vault would be expected to survive the centuries reasonably well, especially as the woods normally used for coffins, either oak or elm, do not decay easily.

This was to be the last occasion the vault was disturbed. *The Times* reported this event, as it had done the opening of the vault in 1813. In a small article at the bottom of column four, page six, of the edition of 17th December, 1888, the following was recorded:

"RELICS OF CHARLES I

The Prince of Wales was on Thursday visiting St. George's Chapel, Windsor, and replaced in the vault containing the coffin of King Charles I, certain relics of that monarch which had been removed during some investigations more than seventy years ago. These relics, having ultimately come into the possession of the Prince of Wales, he decided, with the sanction of the Queen, to replace them in the vault from which they had been taken, but not to disturb the coffin of the King. The Dean of Windsor was present."

XIV EPILOGUE

The execution of King Charles I in 1649 and the subsequent establishment of a Republic under Oliver Cromwell was a fundamental turning-point in British history.

The Civil War achieved three main things. The first was the ending of the ancient feudal rights of the Crown. Secondly the right of the King to levy taxes without the consent of Parliament was destroyed along with the power of the King to arrest members of Parliament without showing proper cause. Thirdly, because Parliament won the wars, it became an unchallengeable part of the English constitution.

The basis of the democracy we have today was born out of the troubles of the seventeenth century and many of the principles established then still hold good.

In 1685, the Duke of Monmouth, the illegitimate but Protestant son of Charles II, raised an army against Catholic James II. In a short, but vicious, campaign the rebel army was soundly defeated, culminating in the last battle to be fought on English soil, at Sedgemoor in Somerset. The Duke of Monmouth was subsequently tried and beheaded.

James was disliked for his Catholicism, but the idea of supporting an illegitimate claimant to the throne, in precedence to the legitimate line of succession, was not considered acceptable.

By 1688 though, James's position was less secure. He openly flaunted his Catholicism and favoured Catholics in the important offices of State. The birth of a male heir and the prospect of a Catholic Stuart dynasty was the last straw and public opinion led Parliament effectively to depose the King who fled the country.

England had had enough of Civil Wars and Rebellions. When William of Orange landed in Brixham, Devon, on 5th November 1688, he was politely treated, but few rushed to support his cause for fear of similar reprisals to those which followed the Monmouth Rebellion. The rebels in the West Country had then been treated severely, with many being tried and either executed or deported. If William was to succeed, he had to do so on his own. Whilst he was not openly supported, more importantly he was unopposed and progressed to London. In the "Glorious Revolution", in which no blood was spilt, the Protestant William and his wife Mary, daughter of James II, were invited by Parliament to become joint monarchs. Parliament was able to negotiate increased authority in the agreement with William and Mary, which effectively ensured the survival of both Parliament and the monarchy, who both now knew clearly their roles in governing the country.

The trial of Charles I shocked Europe at the time, but by the end of the eighteenth century and in the nineteenth century, it was the turn of monarchs in Europe to fall. There was concern in England at the time that the unrest abroad would spread to this country and question again the role of the monarchy here. Everyone was, however, keen to point out that England had already had its revolution. Parliament, the monarchy and, most importantly, the people, were determined that the hard-learnt lessons of history would not allow the country once again to slip into civil war

With the distance of time, we are now able to look dispassionately at the turbulent events of the Civil War. Charles is sometimes seen as a weak King, ill-advised by ineffective Minsters, who were to contribute to the causes of the war. He is seen as obstinate and devious in his negotiations with the Army and with Parliament.

His trial and death marked the end of a troubled reign the effects of which were to change the way this country was governed and which still have an impact on our lives today.

In his manner and bearing in the last days of his life, however, Charles I did much to revive his cause, which ultimately led to the Restoration of the Monarchy in 1660 and saw his son on the throne, as Charles II, as he would have wished.

The actions and dignity of Charles I during his trial and particularly on the scaffold were to impress greatly both friend and foe. The last moments of his life were indeed Charles's finest.

Andrew Marvell, the Puritan poet, in a poem about the King's great enemy, Oliver Cromwell, extolled the virtues of King Charles I ...

> "He nothing common did, or mean,
> Upon that memorable scene,
> but, with his keener eye
> The Axe's edge did try:
> Nor called the Gods with vulgar spite
> To vindicate his helpless Right
> But bow'd his comely head
> Down, as upon a bed."

A fitting epitaph!

50. Statue of Charles I by Hubert de la Soeur at Whitehall,
on the site of the executions of some of the Regicides in the 1660s.

APPENDIX I: THE BANQUETING HOUSE AND THE WINDOW LEADING TO THE SCAFFOLD

There has been much dispute as to which window of the Banqueting House gave access to the scaffold. Many writers may have been misled by contemporary engravings which show some of the windows blocked. Many of these engravings were made by artists who were not themselves present at the execution and who, therefore, had to rely either on hearsay evidence or their own imaginations. The latter is more likely, especially as many of the engravings were produced abroad, where the execution of the King was widely reported. It is commonly held that the window used was the second from the north. Accounts of the time state that the window was specially enlarged for the purpose. This window would have been at the north end of the scaffold, which ran from this window to the sixth window. We know that the scaffold was fairly large, for it accommodated at least fifteen people the next day.

If one looks at the main façade of the Banqueting House today and in particular at the stonework around the windows, there is no visible evidence of any of these windows having been "enlarged", although much of the external stonework may have been replaced over the intervening centuries.

It is difficult to see how any of the main windows could have been enlarged, without the task taking some time and causing significant damage to the stonework. It is equally difficult to see why any of these large windows would have needed to be enlarged.

It may be worth bearing in mind that the Banqueting House was at that time one of Westminster's newest and most prestigious buildings, forming a part of the old rambling medieval Palace of Westminster. The old Palace was large, but there was nowhere suitable for housing the spectacular entertainments which greeted foreign Princes and Ambassadors.

Temporary banqueting houses were constructed of wood and canvas; one such structure, erected by Queen Elizabeth I stood for a quarter of a century, when it was described as being "old and rotten". A more

51. The main façade of the Banqueting House today.

permanent structure of stone was completed in 1607, but was gutted by a fire in 1619.

The present Banqueting House rose on the same site between 1619 and 1623 and was designed in the new "Classical" style by Inigo Jones. It seems odd that such a building would be deliberately damaged, unless it was considered that its extravagant style and the paintings by Rubens glorifying King James symbolised all that was wrong with the Monarchy at the time. Interestingly, the splendid paintings by Rubens decorating the ceiling survived the Civil War and the Commonwealth, despite the fact that they glorified the idea of kingship and the reign of James I.

The Banqueting House today is surrounded by much newer Government buildings, but it is interesting to note that their architectural style shows the obvious influence of Inigo Jones. To anyone unfamiliar with architectural history, the Banqueting House does not look its age and it has survived the Civil Wars and two World Wars unscathed.

Above the entrance to the Banqueting House today is a bronze bust of King Charles and a plaque, marking the site as the place of his execution. The inscription states that a window almost directly above the modern entrance was used. This window no longer exists as it has been blocked and the wall plastered over. The faint outline of what may have been a window can still be seen beneath the plaster, which has some fine surface cracks which follow the original window's outer edge. When viewed from the pavement, this original window is above and slightly to the left of the main door. If there is actually a window beneath this plaster, it

52. The modern entrance to the Banqueting House. This photograph was taken on the anniversary of the execution of King Charles I, hence the wreath hung above the doorway.

cannot be the actual window used by the King, for this part of the Banqueting House, set back some fifteen feet or so from the main façade of the building, is not original.

When built, the Banqueting House was intended to be the first phase of a major improvement to the medieval Palace of Westminster. Only the front and rear façades of the building were decorated; the north and south ends were left plain, as it was the intention that they be joined eventually to other new buildings. The drawing by Hollar shows the north end of the Banqueting House with a temporary brick-built extension containing a staircase. The extension was set only a foot or so back from the main façade of the building and would have been removed and replaced with a more permanent structure when adjoining buildings were added.

When viewed from the front of the Banqueting House, the brick extension to the north contained a door to the Banqueting House, above which was a small window. It was *this* window which was used by the King.

The brick extensions were demolished in 1744 and were replaced by the wider modern entrance we see today. This new extension, like the earlier structure, houses the staircase which leads from the road level up to the Hall. Built probably from brick, the exterior has been rendered to match the colour and appearance of the main building.

An undated (but probably from 1744) and unsigned drawing, now in the British Museum clearly shows the now demolished extension. A much-faded handwritten note states that "King Charles I came through this staircase window to the scaffold. Taken down in 1744."

The drawing clearly shows a small window and it is easy to understand why it would have needed to have been enlarged to make an effective doorway. This "enlarging" may simply have referred to the removal of part or all of the wooden window-frame, which would have been a relatively easy task. The wall in which this window was located was set back a couple of feet from the main façade of the building. As we know, the main part of the scaffold was built in front of the façade. If this window was used, the scaffold must have been "L" shaped, with a small flight of steps required to descend from the window to the level of the scaffold where a short walkway led to the scaffold proper.

There would have been a number of carpenters already on site, engaged in erecting the scaffold who could have removed the window frame and built the steps.

53. Drawing of the original entrance to the Banqueting House. The window marked with an "X" is stated to be the one which Charles used to gain access to the scaffold.

APPENDIX II SIGNATORIES TO THE DEATH WARRANT OF KING CHARLES I

There follows a list of all those who signed the Death Warrant of King Charles I in 1649 and who were, on the Restoration of King Charles II in 1660, known as The Regicides.

The names are listed in the same order as they appear on the Warrant, including the abbreviations to the Christian names where applicable. The one name in italics has been written over an alteration or deletion to whatever name was originally written there.

Jo. Bradshawe	Daniel Bagrave
Tho. Grey	Owen Rowe
O. Cromwell	Will. Porefoy
Edw. Whalley	Ad. Scrope
M. Livesey	James Temple
John Okey	A. Garland
J. Da[n]vers	Edm. Ludlowe
Jo. Bourchier	Henry Marten
H. Ireton	Vinct. Potter
Tho. Mauleverer	Wm. Constable
Har. Waller	Rich. Ingoldsby
John Blakiston	Willi. Cawley
J. Hutchinson	Jo. Barkstead
Willi. Goffe	Isaa. Ewer
Tho. Pride	John Dixwell
Pe. Temple	Valentine Wauton
T. Harrison	Symon Mayne
J. Hewson	Tho. Horton
Hen. Smyth	J. Jones
Per. Pelham	John Moore
Ri. Deane	Gilbt. Millington
Robert Tichbourne	G. Fleetwood
H. Edwardes	J. Alured

Robt. Lilburne
Will. Say
Anth. Stapley
Greg. Norton
Tho. Challoner
Tho. Wogan
John Venn

Gregory Clement
Jo. Downes
Tho. Wayte
Tho. Scot
Jo. Carew
Miles Corbet

APPENDIX III   THE DEATH OF A MONARCH

The funeral arrangements for King Charles I were very different from those which might have been expected for a reigning monarch. It may be useful to digress slightly from the story and see how we would expect to see a seventeenth century monarch buried and ascertain if his burial differs from the norm.

Upon the death of a monarch it was usual at this time for the funeral arrangements to be made by contractors from the College of Arms. After the funeral of Queen Mary in 1694, the role of the College gradually faded from view, as royal burials became private rather than public events.

The first duty of the contractors was the preparation of the body for burial and then making the arrangements for the funeral service and burial.

Since the thirteenth century, the bodies of monarchs had been embalmed as a matter of course. The techniques used were markedly different from those employed by modern embalmers and from those, for example, used by the ancient Egyptians.

The motivation behind the embalming was sanitation not preservation. There was no attempt to preserve the body for religious reasons; it was simply a matter of trying to stop, albeit temporarily, the decomposition of the body.

Embalming at this time seems to have been limited to royal burials and particularly to deceased monarchs. There were specific reasons for this. It was considered essential that the monarch was seen to be dead. This may sound odd to us today, but with poor methods of communication news travelled slowly and rumours were rife. The more people who were able to see the body and verify the fact that the sovereign was in fact dead, the faster the news would travel and, more importantly, the more it would be believed. This was an essential step in ensuring the smooth transition of power to the new monarch, whose reign began the instant the previous incumbent of that position died. Any doubt that the previous monarch was actually dead might seriously disrupt the all-important beginning of the new reign.

On the death of King Henry VIII at Westminster on 28th January, 1547, the body was viewed by members of the Privy Council and others to ensure that he was dead.

It may have also been considered essential for the deceased monarch to be seen in order that, as far as possible, the cause of death could be established as being from natural causes and not as a result of any more sinister activities.

By the mid seventeenth century, these motives might have lost much of their former importance, but by this time embalming had become an accepted practice.

A body will decay very rapidly, and any efforts to limit the extent of the decay, if only for a relatively short term, would be practical, if not essential. Any body, royal or otherwise, would commonly be on view for two or three days after death, to make sure that the deceased was actually deceased. There was a real fear of premature burial until fairly recent times when our better medical knowledge eliminated needless anxiety. Last wills and testaments from the seventeenth century contained instructions that the burial should not be made until a specified number of days after death, giving time for the body to "come back to life again". Other clauses stated that the body should have some of the veins cut open, so in the event of an incorrect diagnosis of death, the supposed deceased would actually become deceased in as pleasant and painless a manner as possible. It must be presumed that evidence of corruption of the body after the requisite number of days would be considered conclusive proof that death had actually occurred.

After one or two days (possibly longer in the cooler months of the year) a body will begin to discolour and smell. Even when placed in a coffin, an unburied body could still become rapidly unpleasant, especially if there was a long delay between death and the funeral. In most instances, burials could be arranged at relatively short notice, but with the death of a monarch, arrangements often took longer. Queen Mary II died in December 1694, but was not actually buried in Westminster Abbey until March 1695. This long delay was not unusual in the circumstances and the time was needed to put into effect the elaborate plans for the funeral, the installation of special seating in the Abbey, the ordering of special suits of mourning for all the guests and even the composition of special music to by played at the funeral service.

This time-delay between death and the funerals of monarchs also determined the construction of the royal coffins. Firstly, however, the body had to be prepared.

The techniques of embalming at this time were relatively simple and would have been performed by the Royal Surgeon or Physician. When

Henry VIII died, word was sent to the surgeons, apothecaries and wax chandlers, "...to do their duties in spurging, cleansing, bowelling, searing, embalming, furnishing and dressing with spices the said corpse."

All clothing would have been removed from the body. *Spurging* was the general washing of the body with spiced and aromatic water to remove the sweat of the death-bed. *Cleansing* was the assisted emptying of the bowels and the plugging of the body orifices. *Bowelling* was the removal of the soft internal organs. An incision was made in the lower abdomen, from the base of the sternum (the breast-bone) to the pelvis. Through this incision, all the soft internal organs were removed. It is these organs which begin to decay first and very soon after death. If not removed they soon become bloated with the production of gasses which can cause the abdomen to swell. In extreme cases a body can, quite literally, explode.

The soft organs, once removed, were placed in a special casket, known as a canopic chest. The chest was sealed immediately and was usually buried in the vault which was later also to hold the body. Accounts of the burial of King Henry VIII mention the burial of the canopic chest in St. George's Chapel. Interestingly, later descriptions of the burial vault containing the coffin of the King make no mention of the presence of any canopic chest. Perhaps in this instance, the coffin and canopic chest were buried in separate locations within the Chapel?

Searing was the cauterising of the body cavity blood vessels and the purification of the body cavity was the technical *embalming*. The empty cavity was cleansed with spirits of wine and was packed with a large amount of material such as sawdust or bran and also sweet smelling herbs. This material would absorb much of the fluid content of the organs. The embalmer's incision was stitched together and the body washed.

Finally, the *furnishing* and *dressing* of the body entailed the application of balms to the body which was then wrapped in a winding sheet.

A winding sheet is simply a large sheet, wrapped or rolled around the body and tied at the head and foot (see illustration 54). The material used is known as cere cloth, which is a very fine cotton which has been impregnated with wax to make it waterproof. At this period bodies were not buried in their everyday clothes. It is, in any event, extremely difficult to dress a body properly and virtually impossible to put on shoes. The shroud, a long shirt-type garment, is a much later funerary fashion.

It is not clear if any attempts were made to drain the blood from the body. There will have been many variations of technique, depending on the knowledge and abilities of the embalmers.

The embalming techniques were not always successful, as is evidenced by the account of the funeral arrangements for King Henry VIII in 1547. The coffin of the King was being taken to Windsor and was laid

54. Monument to John Donne in St. Paul's Cathedral, showing a winding sheet.

overnight at Sion Abbey. The decomposing body began to swell within his coffins and caused them to burst open. The next morning dogs were found consuming some of the fluids which were leaking from the coffins. Henry's vast bulk and gout-infected legs must have presented his embalmers with a difficult task.

Once the body was placed in its coffin the face could, if required, be exposed by untying the end of the winding sheet and rolling the material back. It could easily be tied back into place later. A particularly fine monument survives in St Paul's Cathedral, the only monument there to survive from the old Cathedral destroyed by the Great Fire of London in 1666. It shows Dr. John Donne in a winding sheet. Donne died in 1632 and the funeral effigy was carved by Nicholas Stone.

A large proportion of a body is water, which after death will seep from the body. The sawdust packing of the thoracic cavity of the body would absorb much of the moisture, whilst the wax-impregnated cere cloth would help to contain it. The cloth would also, to a large extent, exclude the air from the body which would help to prevent some decomposition.

The body would have been placed in a wooden coffin. Made of either elm or oak, wooden coffins of the seventeenth century were constructed in exactly the same way as they are today. The panels of the coffins were butt-jointed together and secured by nails. There would often be a "break" or curve in the sides of the coffin at the shoulders, the widest part of the coffin, with the shape of the coffin tapering towards the head and feet. The interior of the coffin was coated with a thick layer of wood pitch, which was melted and painted onto the coffin whilst it was still hot. This pitch made the coffin watertight - not to keep moisture out, but to contain any moisture from the body within the coffin. A thick layer of bran or sawdust covered the bottom of the coffin, which formed a mattress of sorts. A pillow, stuffed with sawdust, wood-shavings or bran was also provided. The pillow prevented the head from dropping back on the floor of the coffin at an unnatural angle. The padding was provided to help absorb any moisture which did escape from the body, as well as to cushion the body and to help to prevent it from moving inside the coffin when it was being carried. A lining of white silk would complete the interior of the coffin. The exterior of the coffin would be left plain and there were no handles provided. The lid was cut to shape and fixed into place by screws.

For the more important burials, a second coffin was then provided and the manufacture of it called upon the skills of the plumbers, for it was made of lead. (The word plumber is derived from the French word for lead, as lead was used extensively for plumbing). "Ten-pound" lead was used, so called because one square foot of the lead sheeting weighed ten pounds. A large sheet of lead would be placed under the wooden coffin and folded up around it. There was no common method of doing this and each plumber would have had his own technique. The excess lead was cut away where it overlapped at the corners of the coffin and the resultant joints were soldered, using molten lead. A lid was made from a separate piece of lead and this too was soldered to the body of the coffin.

The wood coffin was thus completely enveloped in a lead skin. The resultant double coffin may not have looked very elegant, but it would have been both airtight and watertight: watertight to contain any moisture from the body and airtight to contain any unpleasant smells. Once so encapsulated a body could remain unburied until the funerary preparations were complete. The making of such airtight coffins also had a preservative effect on the body within. With the external air excluded, after some initial decay a state of equilibrium of the atmosphere within the coffin would be reached which effectively halted further decay. Lead coffins which have been opened often contain extremely well preserved bodies, with much of the soft tissue surviving. It must be remembered, however, that the preservation of the body was not the reason for the use of such coffins.

The wood and lead coffin was, in turn, contained in a third more elaborate wooden coffin, the construction of which called upon the skills of both the cabinet makers and upholsterers. Made, like the first, of either elm or oak, all the external surfaces of the coffin were covered in black velvet, glued directly onto the surface of the wood. Each part of the rectangular coffin was covered in material separately before being joined to the other component parts.

The edges of these elaborate outer coffins were often decorated with rows of small silver-gilt nails. The nails were used to create ornamental rectangular panels along the sides of the coffin and on the ends. It was usual for there to be three such panels on each of the sides. Each panel would contain a large handle. There would also be a handle fixed at each end of the coffin, making a total of eight handles on the coffin. The weight of a complete set of coffins, with occupant, would have been considerable and it would need six or eight people to carry it.

It was usual for a "breastplate", bearing the name of the deceased and the date of his or her death, to be fixed to the coffin lid, above the chest of the body beneath. On royal coffins this breast-plate would take the form of a crown and, like all the other metal fittings on the coffin, be made of silver-gilt.

The inner wood and lead coffins were lowered into the large outer coffin by heavy webbing tapes. Once fitted together, the webbing could not be removed because of the weight of the inner coffins on it, so the ends of the tapes were simply cut off.

The canopic chests, already mentioned, would have been constructed in the same way as the coffin and would have comprised an inner box of wood, sealed in a lead shell and placed in a more elaborate outer box made of velvet-covered wood.

Interestingly, there had been a major change in the style of coffins in the middle of the seventeenth century. James I was buried in an anthropoid lead coffin. The lead was shaped to fit the body closely and in some cases the surviving coffins even show crude features and faces. James I, who died in 1625, was buried in a small vault in Westminster Abbey containing the bodies of Henry VII (died 1509) and Elizabeth of York (died 1503) and all three bodies are encased in anthropoid coffins. By the 1640s the use of anthropoid coffins had been discontinued. These coffins bear some resemblance to ancient Egyptian anthropoid coffins, and it may be interesting to note that this was the period when the first European travellers were visiting Egypt.

The funeral would have been a great public occasion, with the opportunity to put on a grand show of splendour and pomp. After resting the day before the funeral in the royal bed-chamber, the coffin would be carried in procession to the place of burial. As the body could not be exposed to view, it had become the custom to make elaborate and lifelike funeral effigies of the deceased. Constructed of wood and wax and often wearing clothes the deceased had worn in life, the medieval, Tudor and early Stuart effigies were carried on the bier with the coffin. The surviving later Stuart effigies, from Charles II onwards, were not used as part of the funeral, but appear to have been set up in Westminster Abbey as memorials. Many of these superb royal funeral effigies still survive in Westminster Abbey and they date from medieval times to the early eighteenth century. There is a particularly fine set of Stuart monarchs with effigies of Charles II, William III and Queen Mary and Queen Anne. The features, made of wax, are strikingly lifelike and some of these are likely to be actual death-masks, made shortly after death. The effigies remained on display at the place of burial and replaced any formal stone funeral monuments.

The funeral effigies of both parents of Charles I survive, although both have been damaged badly by the passage of time. The effigy for the funeral of Queen Anne of Denmark was made in 1619. Today only the head and bust survive, but as recently as 1907 it was still attached to the remains of a body made from wood and canvas stuffed with tow (short coarse fibres of flax or hemp). The portrait is stylised but is similar to other portraits of the Queen.

The effigy of James I, who died in 1625, was described at the time as "curiously done and very like him" and it survived the Commonwealth

55. The funeral effigy of Charles II in Westminster Abbey.

period intact. The antiquary George Vertue saw it in the early eighteenth century, although he commented that the head of the effigy, "was recently stolen in 1724/5." Only the wooden body survives today.

The funeral of James I was described by a contemporary, John Chamberlain, as, "..the greatest...ever known in England...the herse likewise beeing the fairest and best fashioned..."

Many of the arrangements for the funeral of King James are preserved in the accounts:

"Abraham Greene. For vessells of lead for Entombeinge of his Royall Corps and bowells.
Abraham Greene for the Entombing of the Royall corps of our late soveraigne King James with lead sodder and workemanship being done at Theobalds. Item more for one vessell of lead to putt in the bowells of his Ryall Majestie with sodder and workemanship."

The Artist Maximilian Colt was paid for the manufacture of the Funeral effigies. It was Colt who had made the effigy of Queen Anne of Denmark. The accounts include items for:

"Paid to Maximilian Colt for makeing the body of the representacion with severall joynts in the armes leggs and body to be moved to severall postures and for setting up the same in Westminster Abbey and for his attendances there. ...*Item* for the face and hands of the said representacion being curiously wrought."

Colt also supplied other items for the funeral which included:

"*Item* for a plate of copper with an inscription fastened upon the breast of the leaden coffin... *Item* for a crowne of wood and a Lyon upon it for his majesties creast... *Item* for a shield with his Majesties armes a garter comptment and a Crowne upon it."

Other entries detail the amounts of cloth purchased for the making of robes for the effigies (Curiously two were made for King James) and for other heraldic banners and shields to be used during the funeral procession and ceremony.

A temporary monument was erected over the burial vault. Designed by the architect Inigo Jones, the structure remained in place for a short time only and was removed soon after the funeral. It contained an elaborate funeral effigy of the King. The accounts of the time detail the costs of the component parts of this monument and include:

The Mausoleum in Westminster Abbey
at the Funeral Obsequies of K. JAMES I.

J. Mynde sc.

56. *The temporary monument to King James I,*
erected in Westminster Abbey immediately after the funeral.

"Item for covering the great hearse in Westminster and for covering and arming all the Pillars and pilasters that suppoerted it: and the others that stood without the hearse all being covered with velvet and garnished with fringes and lace of black silke and also covering all the rayles round about and downe to the ground on both sides."

Clearly the preparations for a Royal funeral took a long time and would have incurred significant expense.

Oliver Cromwell's funeral was based upon that of the last monarch before him to be given a full state funeral, James I. Both were buried in Westminster Abbey. Cromwell was provided with a funeral effigy, showing him in his robes of State. The effigy was destroyed at the time of the Restoration of the Monarchy in 1660.

The royal funerals would have been great heraldic events and special banners and standards would have been carried in procession. Items of funeral armour would have also been provided, including helmets and swords. Many examples still survive, although items from royal funerals are very rare and are limited to items from the funeral of the Black Prince (died 1376) and Henry V (died 1422). A carved, painted and gilded cartouche survives from the funeral of Charles II. It bears the initials C R and the royal crown. The lack of the Roman numerals II between the letters C and R has led some scholars to question whether this item (now in the Museum of London) should be associated with Charles I, but, as we have seen from the accounts of his funeral, this must be considered unlikely.

A painted heraldic panel survives from the funeral hearse of Oliver Cromwell, which is also now in the Museum of London.

The burial would have been made in one of the special vaults constructed beneath the floor of the Cathedral or Abbey chosen as the burial site. For the last five hundred years, most royal burials have been made either at Westminster Abbey or St. Georges's Chapel in Windsor Castle. The vaults were constructed at the heart of the buildings and usually as near to the choir and high altar as possible. One monarch would construct a vault for his use and for that of his family. Some of the vaults are large and most are packed full, as families were large and infant mortality was high.

One of the Stuart vaults in Westminster Abbey, for example, contains the bodies of Henry Prince of Wales (the elder brother of Charles I, who predeceased him), Arabella Stuart, four children of Charles I and Queen Henrietta Maria, Prince Rupert, Queen Elizabeth of Bohemia, ten children of James II and seventeen children of Queen Anne, plus some other members of the Stuart family. When one vault was full, another was constructed.

The entrances to the vaults are beneath the paving slabs of the floor. Whilst they are not always obvious, their whereabouts would have been well known to Abbey officials. Sometimes they had a family name or other inscription on the covering slab. The opening of the vault would be a relatively simple task, when it would be necessary to determine if space remained for any additional burials. If necessary, the earlier burials within the vaults could be moved closer together and it was not unusual for some coffins to be stacked directly on top of the coffins of earlier occupants.

A royal funeral service was always a grand occasion and would be held before a packed congregation, squeezed into additional seating specially provided for the occasion. Anyone with pretensions to a position in society would have wished to be present and all would have clamoured for the best position and view of the proceedings as befitted their rank and status.

After the Reformation, all services were conducted according to the Book of Common Prayer. An exception to this was the funeral of Charles II who died in 1685. The King died a Catholic and was buried remarkably quickly at night during a service which we must presume to have been Catholic. The proceedings were arranged by Charles's brother, the new King James II, who was himself a professed Catholic.

Charles II died on Friday 6th February and his funeral was held in Westminster Abbey on Saturday 14th February. Work to construct a new vault in the Abbey was started on 8th February. The funeral was stripped of the usual pomp. The coffin was surmounted by a royal crown of tin gilt with a cap of crimson velvet turned up with ermine, placed on a blue cushion. The King's coffin was carried from Whitehall to the Abbey under a fringed canopy to the muffled beat of drums.

After burial, it was expected that a suitable monument would be erected above or near the vault, or alternatively, the funeral effigy would be left on display. The last royal funerary monuments to be erected before the reign of Charles I were those of Queen Elizabeth I and of Mary, Queen of Scots; both were erected by Charles's father, James I. James I himself was given no permanent monument and his own place of burial in Westminster Abbey remained unmarked until the nineteenth century. Elaborate funerary monuments remained the norm for the aristocracy throughout the seventeenth and eighteenth century, but for reasons not known to us, the graves of the royal family remained unmarked.

In more normal times, it would have been Charles I's expectation that after his death, his burial would be conducted in the time-honoured manner outlined above as befitted his status as King. What actually happened, as we have already seen, was markedly different.

APPENDIX IV THE SEALED KNOT

The Author has been a member of *The Sealed Knot* for many years. The Society stages a wide variety of seventeenth century historical military re-enactments, throughout the length and breadth of Great Britain. It has a membership of several thousand, which means that it can stage re-enactments of major battles as well as smaller demonstrations of drill and life in soldiers' camps.

The Sealed Knot was founded in 1968 by a distinguished soldier and military historian, the late Brigadier Peter Young, with the object of promoting the study of, and public interest in, the history of the English Civil War. The Society is now Europe's largest and most experienced re-enactment society.

The Badge and Coat of Arms of the Society, granted in 1983, is a device which appears in the collar of the Order of the Garter. The name comes from a Royalist secret society formed in the period of the Commonwealth (1649-1660). The modern Society is non-political and a Registered Charity and includes both Royalists and Parliamentarians within its ranks. New recruits are posted to the ranks and promotion is by merit and ability.

The author joined *The Sealed Knot* as a dragoone in a Royalist regiment, *Prince Maurice's Regiment of Dragoones,* and had the honour of being the Commanding Officer of that regiment for many years, before taking on new roles within the Society. He is now a member of the Heraldic Unit of *The Sealed Knot* and Pageant Master of the Royalist Army.

The Sealed Knot is able to field two large armies, fully equipped, with musket, pike, artillery and cavalry. Through such public performances, the Society has been instrumental in raising funds for many national and local charities, community groups, hospitals, schools and churches.

Whenever possible, in pursuit of its historical objectives, *The Sealed Knot* aims to re-enact the major events associated with the English Civil War on the originals sites and on the actual anniversaries. The Society can recreate the colour, pageantry and spectacle of seventeenth century warfare, with the use of authentic costumes, weapons, formation and tactics. Commentators at the re-enactments put the battles into their correct historical context and explain to the watching audiences the reasons which led to the military engagements and their aftermath. Warfare itself at this time was personal and bloody, and the Society aims to point out the horrors of a Civil War and the disruption and unhappiness it caused in the country.

This period of our history, and the struggle between the King and his Parliament, gave rise to our present form of government. *The Sealed Knot* performs the role of explaining the past on the principle that we can only truly know where we are going if we know and understand where we have been. The motto on the coat of arms granted to *The Sealed Knot* reflects this: "Do well to remember".

57. The Coat of Arms of The Sealed Knot Society

58. 'O Horrable Murder': Contemporary illustration of the execution of Charles I.

BIBLIOGRAPHY

ADAIR, John. *By the Sword Divided*. Century Publishing. 1983.

ASHLEY, Maurice. *Charles II*. Weidenfeld and Nicholson. 1971.

ASHLEY, Maurice. *The English Civil War*. Thames and Hudson. 1980.

AYLMER, G.E. *The King's Servants*. Routledge and Kegan Paul. 1961.

BENCE-JONES, Mark. *The Cavaliers*. Constable and Co. 1976.

BOWLE, John. *Charles the First*. Weidenfeld and Nicholson. 1968.

BROWN, Christopher. *Van Dyck*. Phaidon. 1982.

CARLTON, Charles. *Going to the Wars*. Routledge. 1992.

CHARLTON, John. *The Banqueting House, Whitehall*. H.M.S.O. 1964.

CLARENDON. *History of the Great Rebellion*.

COWIE, Leonard W. *The Trial and Execution of Charles I*. Wayland Publishers. 1972.

FELLOWES, Edmund H. *King Charles I, his Death, his Funeral, his Relics*. Windsor Castle. 1950.

FRASER, Antonia. *King James I*. Book Club Associates. 1974.

GUIZOT, F. *History of the English Revolution*. H.G. Bohn. 1856.

HALFORD, Sir Henry. *Essays and Orations*, including *An account of the opening of the Tomb of King Charles I*. John Murray. 1831.

HARVEY, Anthony and MORTIMER, Richard. *The Funeral Effigies of Westminster Abbey*. The Bogdell Press. 1994.

HAYTHORNTHWAITE, Philip. *The English Civil War*. Blandford Press. 1983.

HERBERT, Sir Thomas. *Memoirs*. In *The Trial of Charles I*. Editor Roger Lockier. The Folio Society. 1959.

HIBBERT, Christopher. *Charles I*. Weidenfeld and Nicholson. 1975.

HIGHAM, F.M.G. *Charles I*. Hamish Hamilton. 1932.

JONES, Jack D. *The Royal Prisoner*. Lutterworth Press. 1965.

LITTEN, Julian. *The English Way of Death*. Robert Hole. 1992.

MANSFIELD, Alan. *Ceremonial Costume*. Adam and Charles Black. 1980.

MILLER, Oliver. *Van Dyck in England*. National Portrait Gallery. 1982.

MORGAN, Kenneth O. (Editor). *The Oxford Illustrated History of Britain*. Guild Publishing. 1984.

MORRAH, Patrick. *A Royal Family*. Constable. 1982.

MUDDIMAN, J.G. *The Trial of King Charles the First*. Wm. Hodge and Co. 1928.

NEWMAN, Peter R. *Companion to the English Civil Wars*. Fact on File. 1990.

OLLARD, Richard. *This War without an Enemy*. Atheneum. 1976.

PLUMB, J.H. *Royal Heritage*. B.B.C. 1977.

RIDLEY, Jasper. *The Roundheads*. Constable and Co. 1976.

ROCHE, E.W.E. *Henrietta of Exeter*. Phillmore. 1971.

ROOTS, Ivan. "Cromwell's Head". Article from the University Of Exeter Magazine. 1985.

RUSHWORTH, John. *Memoirs*. In *The Trial of Charles I*. Editor Roger Lockier. The Folio Society. 1959.

TAYLOR, I.A. *The Life of Queen Henrietta Maria*. Hutchinson and Co. 1904.

WARDON, Blair (Editor). *Stuart England*. Phaidon. 1986.

WATSON, D.R. *The Life and Times of Charles I*. Weidenfeld and Nicholson. 1972.

WEDGWOOD, C.V. *The King's Peace*. Collins/Fontana. 1955.

WEDGWOOD, C.V. *The King's War*. Collins/Fontana. 1958.

WEDGWOOD, C.V. *The Trial of Charles I*. Wm. Collins. 1964.

WEDGWOOD, C.V. *Oliver Cromwell*. Corgi. 1975.

WICKHAM, D.E. *Discovering Kings and Queens*. Shire Publications. 1973.

WREN SOCIETY. *The Fifth Volume of the Wren Society*. Oxford. 1928.

YOUNG, Peter. *Edgehill 1642*. Roundwood Press. 1967.

YOUNG, Peter. *Naseby 1645*. Century Publishing. 1985.

YOUNG, Peter and HOLMES, Richard. *The English Civil War*. Eyre Methuen. 1974.

INDEX